TROY

Randy Alcorn

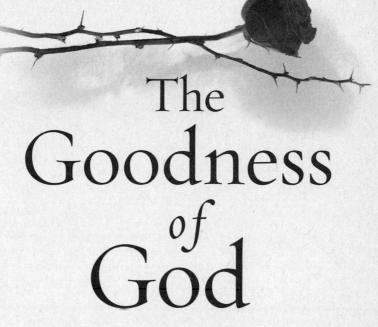

The Goodness of God

Assurance *of* Purpose
in the Midst *of* Suffering

MULTNOMAH
BOOKS

THE GOODNESS OF GOD
PUBLISHED BY MULTNOMAH BOOKS
12265 Oracle Boulevard, Suite 200
Colorado Springs, Colorado 80921

All Scripture quotations, unless otherwise indicated, are taken from the Holy Bible, New International Version®. NIV®. Copyright © 1973, 1978, 1984 by International Bible Society. Used by permission of Zondervan Publishing House. All rights reserved. Scripture quotations marked (ESV) are taken from The Holy Bible, English Standard Version, © 2001 by Crossway Bibles, a division of Good News Publishers. Used by permission. All rights reserved. Scripture quotations marked (KJV) are taken from the King James Version. Scripture quotations marked (NASB) are taken from the New American Standard Bible®. © Copyright The Lockman Foundation 1960, 1962, 1963, 1968, 1971, 1972, 1973, 1975, 1977, 1995. Used by permission. (www.Lockman.org). Scripture quotations marked (NLT) are taken from the Holy Bible, New Living Translation, copyright © 1996, 2004. Used by permission of Tyndale House Publishers Inc., Wheaton, Illinois 60189. All rights reserved.

Italics in Scripture quotations reflect the author's added emphasis.

ISBN 978-1-60142-343-6
ISBN 978-1-60142-353-5 (electronic)

Portions of this book have been adapted from *If God Is Good: Faith in the Midst of Suffering and Evil,* © 2009 by Eternal Perspective Ministries.

Published in the United States by WaterBrook Multnomah, an imprint of the Crown Publishing Group, a division of Random House Inc., New York.

MULTNOMAH and its mountain colophon are registered trademarks of Random House Inc.

Library of Congress Cataloging-in-Publication Data
Alcorn, Randy C.
    The goodness of God : assurance of purpose in the midst of suffering / Randy Alcorn.—
1st ed.
        p. cm.
    Shorter, rewritten with new material of author's earlier work: If God is good.
    ISBN 978-1-60142-343-6 (alk. paper)—ISBN 978-1-60142-353-5 (electronic : alk. paper)
1. Theodicy. 2. Suffering—Religious aspects—Christianity. 3. God (Christianity)—Goodness. I. Alcorn, Randy C. If God is good— II. Title.
    BT160.A418 2010
    231'.8—dc22
                                        2010008694

Printed in the United States of America
2010

10 9 8 7 6 5 4 3 2

SPECIAL SALES
Most WaterBrook Multnomah books are available at special quantity discounts when purchased in bulk by corporations, organizations, and special interest groups. Custom imprinting or excerpting can also be done to fit special needs. For information, please e-mail SpecialMarkets@WaterBrookMultnomah.com or call 1-800-603-7051.

To Doreen Button, Thomas Womack,
Pamela Shoup, and Holly Briscoe,
with deep appreciation for your editorial skills.

Contents

I know the things that happen: the loss and the loneliness and the pain.... But there's a mark on it now: as if Someone who knew that way Himself, because He had travelled it, had gone on before and left His sign; and all of it begins to make a little sense at last—gathered up, laughter and tears, into the life of God, with His arms around it!

—Paul Scherer

Introduction

A Search We All Share

During the two years it took to research and write my large book *If God Is Good: Faith in the Midst of Suffering and Evil,* many people asked me what I was working on. I expected my answer—containing the words *evil* and *suffering*—would prompt a quick change of subject. Most, however, expressed keen interest and asked penetrating questions. Several launched into their own stories, as if having received permission to uncork the bottle.

What, after all, is more universal to human experience than suffering? And what can be more important than the perspective we bring to it?

WHEN IT'S DEEPLY PERSONAL

You may be looking for answers to a philosophical problem or an intellectual struggle. Or you may be looking less for answers than for hope. When a child has fallen off a bicycle, her father doesn't give a lecture about nerve endings, skin tissue, and the role of blood as it's pumped by the heart. He reassures the child that he's there for her, and "everything will be okay." For you, the answer may simply be "God really does love me."

If something like abuse, desertion, debilitating disease, or the loss of a loved one has devastated you, then suffering isn't theoretical or philosophical. It's deeply personal.

In writing his magnificent story of redemption, God has revealed truths about himself, us, the world, goodness, evil, suffering, and Heaven and Hell. Those truths teem with life—the blood of man and of God flows through them. God speaks with passion, not indifference. To come to grips with the problem of evil and suffering, you must do more than hear heart-wrenching stories about suffering people. You must hear God's truth to help you interpret those stories.

Maybe you're holding on to years of bitterness and depression. You blame someone else for your suffering—and that someone may be God. You will not find relief unless you gain perspective.

But perhaps you fear that any attempt to "gain perspective" will deny or minimize your suffering, or that of others. I promise you, the Bible doesn't minimize suffering or gloss over it, and neither will I.

At times, each of us must snuggle into our Father's arms, like children, and there receive the comfort we need. God doesn't just offer us advice, he offers us companionship. He doesn't promise we won't face hardship, but he does promise he'll walk with us through our hardship.

The Question

A Barna Research poll asked, "If you could ask God only one question and you knew he would give you an answer, what would you ask?" The most common response was, "Why is there pain and suffering in the world?"[1] This isn't merely *a* problem; it's *the* problem. And for the culture at large, it appears to pose a greater difficulty now than ever. Unlike the average person in earlier centuries, we today have a far higher assumption and expectation of comfort, health, and prosperity.

When people take time to reflect on life's meaning in this world, no question looms larger than this one: If God is good...*why all this evil and suffering*? If God loves us, how can he justify allowing (or sending) the sometimes overwhelming difficulties we face? How we answer this question will radically affect how we perceive God and the world around us.

We may want to turn away from the world's suffering and ignore the significance of our own pain; we just want it to go away. But despite the superficiality of our culture, we remain God's image-bearers— thinking and caring people, wired to ask questions and seek answers.

You won't get far in a conversation with someone who rejects the Christian faith before the problem of evil is raised. Atheists such as Richard Dawkins and Christopher Hitchens claim it proves that God doesn't exist. (Never mind that many who suffer most believe and trust in God, while many who suffer least don't.) British philosopher Antony Flew, a former champion of atheism, renounced his atheism during the past decade, citing the complexity of the universe and his belief in the overwhelming evidence for intelligent design. Flew did not, however, convert to the Christian faith, but only to deism. Why? He couldn't get past the problem of evil. He believes God must have created the universe, then abandoned it.

MY OWN EXPERIENCES WITH SUFFERING

I'm a fellow traveler with you on this road of suffering. In 1970, as a sixteen-year-old new Christian, I watched my friend Greg die from a horrible accident. In 1979, I had to tell my mother that her only brother had been murdered with a meat cleaver. Two years later, Mom died from cancer. About the same time, I was in the throes of an unjust lawsuit that cost me a job I loved and the ability to earn a normal wage.

In 1992 I was alone with my best friend from childhood when he died from cancer, at age thirty-nine. A few years later—alongside my wife, daughters, and brother—I held my dad's hand as he died, a shriveled version of the vibrant man I'd known.

For twenty-five years I've battled a disease that daily affects my body and mind, and will probably shorten my life span. But all in all, if I've suffered a little more than some people, I've suffered a great deal less than others. And while seeking to understand the huge question of evil and suffering, I've realized my need for a deeper and wider perspective.

Along the way I've asked God to give me wisdom—and discovered that wisdom begins with the humility to say, "There's a great deal about this I don't understand." In fact, if I imagined I had all the answers neatly lined up, what I've written wouldn't be worth reading.

While researching this subject, I've read nearly a hundred books, listened to countless lectures and debates, and interviewed dozens of people who have faced great evil and suffering. That probably doesn't sound like fun, yet I found something surprising: the journey was not only rewarding, but also fascinating, enlightening, and at times downright enjoyable. I know it sounds counterintuitive—shouldn't meditating on evil and suffering be *depressing*? In fact, I'd already seen enough evil and suffering to feel deeply troubled. What I needed was *perspective.*

In my search for answers, I've beheld the God who says, "I have indeed seen the misery of my people.… I have heard them crying out…and I am concerned about their suffering" (Exodus 3:7). I revel in God's emphatic promise in the Bible that he will make a New Earth where he'll come down to live with his people, where "he will wipe every tear from their eyes," and "there will be no more death or mourning or crying or pain" (Revelation 21:4).

Often, as I've contemplated potentially faith-jarring situations, God has wiped away my own tears as I've sought his truth. While my journey hasn't unearthed easy answers, I'm astonished at how much insight the Bible offers on this most troubling of all subjects. And after much wrestling with the issues, instead of being disheartened, I'm encouraged—especially from seeing so much of God's goodness, love, holiness, justice, patience, grace, and mercy.

This journey has stretched my trust in God and his purposes, and I've emerged better prepared to face suffering and to help others who suffer. I feel I have much more to offer believers in Christ who may be questioning their faith, as well as unbelievers who consider the problem of evil and suffering their single greatest obstacle to faith. With that in mind, I invite you to join me on this journey that I've found so interesting, enlightening, and ultimately comforting.

WHEN LOSING FAITH IS *GOOD*

Evil and suffering have a way of exposing our inadequate theology. When affliction comes, a weak or nominal Christian often discovers that his faith doesn't account for it or prepare him for it. His faith has been in his church, denomination, or family tradition, or in his own religious ideas—but not in Christ. As he faces evil and suffering, he may, in fact, lose his faith.

But that's actually a good thing; any faith that leaves us unprepared for suffering is a false faith that deserves to be abandoned.

Genuine faith will be tested by suffering; false faith will be lost— the sooner, the better.

Believing God exists isn't the same as *trusting* the God who exists. If you base your faith on lack of affliction, your faith lives on the brink of extinction and will fall apart because of a frightening diagnosis or a shattering phone call. As John Piper writes, "Wimpy Christians won't survive the days ahead."[2]

Only when you jettison ungrounded and untrue faith can you replace it with valid faith in the true God—faith that can pass, and even find strength in, the most formidable of life's tests.

Unfortunately, most churches have failed to teach people to think biblically about the realities of evil and suffering. A pastor's daughter told me, "I was never taught the Christian life was going to be difficult. I've discovered it is, and I wasn't ready."

Our failure to teach a biblical theology of suffering leaves Christians unprepared for harsh realities. It also leaves our children vulnerable to history, philosophy, and global studies classes that raise the problems of evil and suffering while denying the Christian worldview. Since the question *will* in fact be raised, shouldn't Christian parents and churches raise it first and take people to Scripture to see what God says about it?

No Quick Fix

You'll notice in these pages that I frequently quote Scripture. I do so because God promises that his Word "will not return to me empty, but will accomplish what I desire and achieve the purpose for which I sent it" (Isaiah 55:11). God never makes this promise about my words or yours. That's why I'm convinced that this book can accomplish God's purpose only if it remains faithful to his words.

As you read along, I urge you not to let your feelings—real as they are—invalidate your need to let the truth of God's words guide your thinking. Remember that the path to your heart travels through your mind. *Truth matters.*

So as you deal with suffering, by all means speak with a friend or pastor or counselor, or join a support group. Do not, however, ignore truth in the process. Quick-fix feelings will never sustain you over the long haul. But deeply rooted beliefs—grounded in Scripture—will allow you to persevere and hold on to a faith built on the solid rock of God's truth.

Drenched in his own tears, the prophet Habakkuk said,

How long, O LORD, must I call for help,
    but you do not listen?
Or cry out to you, "Violence!"
    but you do not save?
Why do you make me look at injustice?
    Why do you tolerate wrong? (1:2–3)

By including this and many similar laments in his inspired Word, God graciously invites our cries—so long as we remain willing to listen to his response.

The root issue behind Habakkuk's cry—and behind our own similar questioning—is a problem that people have expressed in various ways, with different nuances. I'll state it this way:

If God is all-good and all-knowing and all-powerful, why is there so much evil and suffering in the world? Surely he wants to prevent it, knows how to prevent it, and has the ability to prevent it.

So why doesn't he?

Notes
1. Lee Strobel, *The Case for Faith* (Grand Rapids, MI: Zondervan, 2000), 29.
2. John Piper, *Spectacular Sins* (Wheaton, IL: Good News, 2008), 57.

1

Tragic Choices

Determining the Origins of Evil and Suffering

His teenage son had died three months earlier. Randy Butler was a pastor I met while teaching a seminary course on the theology of Heaven. After the class, he said, "For twenty years, God gave me a perfect life, family, and ministry. Then Kevin died, and nearly every morning, for three or four months, I screamed questions at God: *What were you thinking?… Is this the best you can do for me?… Do you really expect me to show up every Sunday and tell everyone how great you are?*

"In the silence I began to hear the voice of God…then, without any announcement, when I became silent, God spoke to my soul. He had an answer for each of my three questions."

Had Randy not been painfully honest with God, he might never have come to such an understanding. He might never have realized that he wasn't the first father to watch his son die. More than anyone in the universe, God understood Randy's pain—because he had endured the death of his own Son. DOES SCRIPTURE SPEAK TO GOD'S GRIEF

God knows it and we know it—*things are not all right with the world.* But what does that mean?

Why Evil Is Evil

The pain of suffering points to something deeply and unacceptably flawed about this world we inhabit. We instinctively sense a link between suffering and evil. But how do we explain it?

Evil is a fundamental departure from goodness. The Bible uses the word *evil* to describe anything that violates God's moral will. The first human evil occurred when Eve and Adam disobeyed God. From that first sin—a moral evil—came the consequence of suffering.

Moral evil includes blatant wickedness that admits its hatred for goodness, and subtle malevolence that professes to love goodness while violating it.

Whenever we attempt to liberate ourselves from God's standards and replace them with our own, we not only deny God but affirm ourselves as god. We commit the idolatry of self. Evildoers not only reject God's Law and create their own, they often attempt to take the moral high ground by calling God's standards "unloving," "intolerant," and "evil."

Most people today understand evil as anything that harms others; the more harm done, the more evil the action. The Bible uses the word *evil* in a broader way to describe anything that flows not from loving God but rebelling against him.

This evil is more than merely the absence of good, though some people view it that way—just as darkness is the absence of light, and death is the taking away of life. New Testament vocabulary can sometimes support this concept, in words such as *un*righteous, *un*just, *un*godly, law*less,* and god*less.* These suggest that we best understand evil as a departure from God's goodness. However, while this definition contains helpful insights, it doesn't go far enough.

The Holocaust was not "nothing." The Killing Fields were not "nothing." The 9/11 attacks were not "nothing." All were real horrors, down to every emaciated corpse, bullet-riddled body, and person jumping out a window.

✶ Evil cannot exist without the good it opposes. It's not so much the removal of good as it is the *corruption* of good. As metal does not need rust, but rust needs metal, so good doesn't need evil, but evil needs good.

We can think of evil as a parasite on God's good creation. Without the living organism it uses as a host, the parasite cannot exist. Likewise, cancer thrives on, consumes, and ultimately kills healthy, living cells. Evil's corruption eats away at everything around it.

We see this most tragically in Genesis 3, when the first human evil occurred as Eve and Adam disobeyed God. That first sin unloosed the ever-expanding consequences of suffering. So suffering follows evil as a caboose follows an engine.

As the moral evil of rebellion against God breeds suffering everywhere, these resulting calamities and tragic events are sometimes also referred to in Scripture as evils themselves. We can therefore think of two kinds of evil—moral wrongdoing as *primary evil,* and suffering as *secondary evil.* Primary evils are things *we* do that *God* doesn't like; they're the cause of secondary evils, which are things that happen *to* us that *we* don't like.

✗ As the direct and indirect consequences of primary evil, secondary evil provokes our indignation: *why do innocent people suffer?* However, by pointing to primary evil, secondary evils remind us that sinful humanity deserves suffering.

As humans, we all stand guilty. Although many secondary evils befall us even when we have not directly committed a sin that causes them, we would not have to deal with secondary evils if we didn't belong to a sinful race.

Short-term suffering serves as a warning and a foretaste of eternal suffering. Without a taste of Hell, we would not see its horrors nor feel much motivation to do everything possible to avoid it. Hence, the secondary evil of suffering can get our attention and prompt us to repent of our primary moral evil.

But how did such a terrible situation come about in the first place?

THIS IS NOT HOME

How the Rebellion Began

The evil of rebellion against God is something that entered the universe through Satan, then through the fallen angels.

It's misleading to say, "God created Satan and demons." Rather, God created Lucifer and other righteous angels, who later <u>chose to rebel against God</u>, and in so doing *became* Satan and demons.

The great archangel who rebelled against his Creator is called the devil (which means "slanderer") and Satan ("accuser"). Jesus called him "a liar and the father of lies" and a "murderer from the beginning" (John 8:44). Christ also referred to him as "the evil one" (Matthew 13:19) and "the prince of this world" (John 12:31; 14:30; 16:11).

Satan and the demons dreamed of having authority over themselves and exalting themselves above God. They sinned by desiring to have more power than God had appointed to them.

Satan's work is evil and suffering, and that's exactly what the Messiah came to ultimately defeat: "The reason the Son of God appeared was to destroy the devil's work" (1 John 3:8). From the beginning, God planned that his Son should deal the death blow to

Satan, evil, and suffering—reversing the Curse triggered by Adam and Eve's sin, redeeming a fallen humanity, and repairing a broken world.

WHO IS GOD'S EQUAL?

As Satan instigates evil and suffering in our lives, we must remember that he is not God's opposite; the two are not fighting a cosmic duel with an uncertain outcome.

When asked to name the opposite of God, people often answer, "Satan." But that's false. Michael, the righteous archangel, is Satan's opposite. Satan is finite; God is infinite. God has no equal.

It's true that Satan and demons have great power, and we dare not underestimate it. Satan inflicts evil and suffering on both the world and God's people. He's like "a roaring lion looking for someone to devour" (1 Peter 5:8).

But Satan poses no threat to God. Therefore we're told, "Submit yourselves…to God. Resist the devil, and he will flee from you" (James 4:7). We should never quote the last part of that verse without the first: *submit yourselves to God.* That alone is the basis upon which we, who are no match for Satan, can successfully resist him.

It shouldn't surprise us when Satan uses evil and suffering—the very things he specializes in—to get us to question God's goodness, love, power, or knowledge. His purpose in all he does is to keep us from trusting our Savior. Just as he did with Eve, he wants us to question God's Word: "Did God *really* say that?"

Satan's attacks on us, however, are only within God's set limits. Jesus said to Peter, "Satan demanded to have you, that he might sift you like wheat" (Luke 22:31, ESV). The devil sought to destroy Peter's faith, but he could bring into Peter's life only what the all-knowing and all-powerful God gave him permission to bring. God has veto power over Satan. Satan is a lion seeking to devour us, yet he remains a lion on God's leash. One day we'll each learn how many times God refused Satan's requests to bring greater temptations and hardships upon us.

⭐ Although the Bible points to Satan and the fallen angels as the entry of evil into our universe, evil's ultimate origin remains a mystery. Scripture addresses *when* evil came into being, but not *how*. Deuteronomy 29:29 seems to apply here: "The secret things belong to the LORD our God." He has chosen to remain silent on this question, which may itself be significant. If evil is irrational, how can its point of origin be rationally explained? Perhaps God doesn't offer any explanation because evil defies explanation. It might make sense to an all-knowing God but no sense at all to us.

What's easier for us to understand is the account of how Adam and Eve fell after being tempted by an evil being.

WHERE OUR PAIN BEGAN

After God declared his creation "very good," he gave Adam and Eve these instructions: "You are free to eat from any tree in the garden; but you must not eat from the tree of the knowledge of good and evil, for when you eat of it you will surely die" (Genesis 1:31; 2:16–17).

Even with this clear warning, the first human couple weighed their alternatives, and evil somehow entered their hearts. Adam and Eve rebelled, choosing to violate God's explicit command. They ate what was forbidden. The Curse fell upon them, their pain greatly increased, the Earth became a world of hurt, and they forfeited paradise.

Grievous as it was, Adam and Eve's sin <u>did not take God by surprise.</u> Though evil had no part in God's original creation, it was fully anticipated in his original plan. That original plan was decided in eternity past, and it included Christ's death on the cross to pay the penalty for our sin. Jesus is "the Lamb that was slain *from the creation of the world*" (Revelation 13:8); likewise, God "chose us in him [Christ] *before the creation of the world*" and "*predestined* us to be adopted as his sons through Jesus Christ" (Ephesians 1:4–5). From the perspective of a timeless God, Christ's sufferings and death did not confine themselves to a few years or hours. Before the world fell—even before he created it—God knew *exactly* what he would do to redeem the world. He knew the horrors of evil before Adam and Eve knew them.

This tells us that God didn't devise his redemptive plan on the fly after Adam and Eve stumbled. From before the very beginning, God knew the very worst—as well as the very best it would one day bring.

What Our Choices Are

God didn't *force* Adam and Eve to do evil, but he did create them with freedom of choice. He also permitted Satan's presence in the <u>Garden of Eden,</u> fully knowing Adam and Eve would choose evil.

The Bible attributes the origin of all human evil to people's choices. When we choose to disobey God's standards, it inevitably brings suffering. To argue that God should not permit such evil or suffering is to argue against human beings having real choice—or to insist that our choices be inconsequential, and therefore meaningless. The problem of evil is therefore the problem of freedom. Without freedom there could be no evil.

Imagine removing meaningful choice from your springer spaniel. What would be left might be a dog who doesn't chew your slippers or chase the neighbor's cat, who doesn't bark or growl. But he also doesn't crawl in your lap and beg you to scratch him. He doesn't snuggle up to you or pull you out the door by his leash and lead you through the neighborhood, exploring. In other words, what you have left may look like a dog, but he would no longer be a dog. If that is true of an animal, how much more is it true of a human being?

God isn't the author of evil, but he *is* the author of a story that includes evil. He intended from the beginning to permit evil, then to turn it on its head—to take what fallen angels and fallen people intended for evil and use it for good. In the face of the worst wrongs, God intended to show his highest good.

The Fall, the first human tragedy, became the mother of all subsequent ones. We should do nothing to minimize it or to pretend it mattered less than it did. Yet the Fall did *not* end God's plan for humanity. As we'll come to see more clearly, God would ultimately use evil to accomplish the greater end of redemption in Christ. God could hate evil and yet permit it in order to carry out an astounding, far-reaching redemptive plan in Christ, one that would forever overshadow the evil and sufferings of this present world.

WHO CAUSES NATURAL DISASTERS?

Earthquakes and tsunamis are not moral agents and therefore cannot be morally evil. A tidal wave is not malicious—water cannot have malice any more than it can have kindness.

The best answer to the question, "Why would God create a world with natural disasters?" is that he *didn't*. Many experts believe the world's atmosphere originally acted like an umbrella, protecting its inhabitants from harm. But humanity's fall and the curse that followed it put holes in that umbrella. Sometimes it still protects us, sometimes not.

People who have survived disasters often say they understand on a far deeper level the biblical truth that this world *as it now is*—under the Curse—is not our home.

Natural disasters ordinarily are general results of the Curse, *not* specifically linked to the sins of individuals who perish or suffer in them. Regarding the southeast Asian tsunami, the Haitian earthquake, African famines, the man born blind (see John 9), or the sufferings of Job, unless God reveals it in his Word, it is a mistake to declare that God is bringing judgment on specific people because of their specific sins. After all, the Bible shows that the righteous often suffer in this world, and the unrighteous often prosper.

Suppose a king built a fabulous estate with beautiful gardens—his whole country was the most beautiful place in the world. But an invading army came in and savaged it, tearing apart the gardens, cutting down the trees, enslaving the servants. If someone came from a far country in search of this great land they'd heard of, they would say, "If there is a good and wise king, surely he would have made a better place than this." You try to explain that there is indeed a good and wise king and he did make a far better place. And that he has not given up on it, but is marshaling his forces and will come back to conquer and reclaim his country. But the man looks at you skeptically, because he judges based on only what he sees now.

Human beings were created by God to be faithful stewards of the Earth, but the Curse, brought about by their rebellion against him (see Genesis 3:17), has disrupted natural forces and extends to everything in the natural world, making it harder for people to live productively. The Bible says that creation has been "subjected to frustration" by

God's curse, until that day when "the creation itself will be liberated from its bondage to decay" (Romans 8:20–21). The next verse says, "The whole creation has been groaning as in the pains of childbirth." Earthquakes, volcanoes, and tsunamis reflect the frustration, bondage, and decay of an earth groaning under sin's curse.

This tragic cause-and-effect relationship between man's wrongdoings and nature's malfunctioning points to the disastrous consequences of turning away from God. In a universe designed by God and reflective of his nature, *sin produces bad consequences.*

In fact, our sinful actions often make the Earth's cursed condition even worse. Fatalities in natural disasters can multiply because of morally evil human actions. People frequently build houses in areas long proven vulnerable to floods, landslides, wildfires, tornadoes, and earthquakes. Some perish when they refuse warnings to vacate their homes.

Humans misuse land, resulting in disastrous mudslides. Polluted rivers and air can cause deaths, sickness, and physical deformities. Sometimes more people suffer losses from looting following a hurricane than in the hurricane itself. People may fail to generously share their God-given resources to rescue the needy. In some disaster-stricken countries, government leaders may hoard outside aid sent to help their suffering people.

Natural disasters aren't inherently evil, but they can produce secondary evils by thwarting what's best for humanity as well as the environment. They become most disastrous when they take human life—something that never happened until after humans first committed moral evil against God.

Time after time throughout history, God has used both man-made and natural disasters to draw people to himself. Philosophy professor Eleonore Stump wrote,

I HAVEN'T DONE THIS.

Natural evil—the pain of disease, the intermittent and unpredictable destruction of natural disasters, the decay of old age, the imminence of death—takes away a person's satisfaction with himself. It tends to humble him, show him his frailty, make him reflect on the transience of temporal goods, and turn his affections towards other-worldly things, away from the things of this world.[1]

When we face a natural disaster, a disease, or even a financial hardship, we should ask our sovereign God, "What are you trying to tell us?"

☆ Disasters can initiate people's self-examination and bring out the best in them. A world without personal tragedy or natural disasters would produce no heroes.

Whenever we're tempted to think God has messed up our nice world by interjecting evil and suffering into it, let's remember that in fact *we* messed up God's perfect world by interjecting evil and suffering. Then he came down and suffered evil by our hands so that we could forever be delivered from evil and suffering and death. Rather than blaming or resenting God, we should be overwhelmed with gratitude that if we trust his redemptive work on our behalf, then our suffering is only temporary and not eternal.

CHOOSING GOODNESS OVER EVIL

God wants the difference between good and evil to remain crystal-clear to us.

It's bad enough to do evil and abstain from good. But God condemns the moral sleight of hand by which we so often confuse good and evil: "Woe to those who call evil good and good evil, who put darkness for light and light for darkness, who put bitter for sweet and sweet for bitter" (Isaiah 5:20).

God says, "Hate what is evil; cling to what is good" (Romans 12:9). These passages presume we know the difference between good and evil. But in a culture that so often switches the price tags so what's valuable looks worthless and what's cheap demands a high price, this doesn't come naturally. <u>We must regularly withdraw to Scripture and ask God's Spirit to train our minds and consciences to recognize what's truly good and what's truly evil.</u>

Meanwhile, as we face life's challenges and disasters, we should seek to see God's hand on our lives and to trust him to fulfill his promise to work "all things"—including evil and suffering—"together for good to those who love God" (Romans 8:28, NASB). Joni Eareckson Tada and Steve Estes express that hard-to-believe-but-emphatically-promised-by-God truth this way:

> God cares most—not about making us comfortable—but about teaching us to hate our sins, grow up spiritually, and love him. To do this, he gives us salvation's benefits only gradually, sometimes painfully gradually. In other words, he lets us continue to feel much of sin's sting while we're headed for heaven…where at last, every sorrow we taste will one day prove to be the best possible thing that could have happened.[2]

Notes

1. Eleonore Stump and Michael J. Murray, *Philosophy of Religion* (Hoboken, NJ: Wiley-Blackwell, 1999), 233.
2. Joni Eareckson Tada and Steven Estes, *When God Weeps* (Grand Rapids, MI: Zondervan, 1997), 56.

2

What's Wrong? I Am

Accepting the Reality of Inherited Sin

I n his twenties, John Newton commanded eighteenth-century English slave ships. Sometimes a quarter of the slaves died on the journey. In his earlier years, Newton blasphemed God and engaged in brutality and immorality. He prided himself on being incorrigible.

When he eventually left the slave trade, growing in a new faith in Christ, he felt increasing remorse for what he'd done. For the last half of his life he pastored a church near London, where he preached the gospel, taught the Scriptures, and eventually spoke out against the slave trade, encouraging young parliamentarian William Wilberforce in his battle to outlaw slavery.

At age eighty-two, shortly before his death, a physically blind and spiritually sighted John Newton said, "My memory is nearly gone, but I remember two things: That I am a great sinner, and that Christ is a great Saviour."[1]

Newton wrote hundreds of hymns, the most famous of which is the most popular song among many African Christians throughout the world:

Amazing grace! How sweet the sound
That saved a wretch like me,

I once was lost, but now am found,
Was blind, but now I see.

Newton's claim to wretchedness wasn't hyperbole; he clearly saw his own evil within. While Newton may appear an extreme case, the Bible teaches that all of us are evil-lovers and evildoers, blind wretches in desperate need of God's transforming grace.

OUTRAGEOUS OFFENSES

We tend to minimize our sin because we fail to see its real object. When we hurt those we love, we become aware of our sin because their obvious pain reflects our evil back to us like a mirror. But since we don't see God or observe how our sin hurts him, we fail to realize both the frequency and the gravity of our offenses. We imagine our sin has little or no effect on him. We couldn't be more wrong.

D. A. Carson writes, "Evil is evil because it is rebellion against God. Evil is the failure to do what God demands or the performance of what God forbids.... The dimensions of evil are thus established by the dimensions of God; the ugliness of evil is established by the beauty of God; the filth of evil is established by the purity of God; the selfishness of evil is established by the love of God."[2]

Those who have committed adultery often feel profoundly the consequences of their evil as they see the faces of their spouses, children, and friends. They may feel deep sorrow for the hurt they've brought. But sometimes they fail to see their primary sin against God. And when we fail to see that we have sinned against God above all—the One who has maximum worthiness—then no matter how bad we feel about what we've done to others, we will inevitably minimize our sin.

The man who commits adultery does not just trespass against his wife and children. He violates the standards of the God before whom angels cry out, "Holy, holy, holy" (Isaiah 6:3). Repentance without recognizing our offense against God is not repentance.

Our sin natures mean that, generally, "Be yourself" is not good advice.

In his words of confession to God in Psalm 51, David rightly recognizes the very definition of sin when he tells God he has "done *what is evil in your sight*" (verse 4). But with Bathsheba, David had sinned against his friend, his family, and his nation. Why then in that same verse does he say, "Against you, you only, have I sinned"? I think David is correcting in himself the tendency we all have—to limit our sorrow to the hurt we've inflicted on human beings, and to overlook God's perspective.

INHERITED SIN

The term *inherited sin* speaks of our moral condition resulting from the Fall—our condition of inborn sinfulness leading inescapably to death. Various scriptures tell us that we're "sinful at birth," that "from birth" we "go astray," that "the many died by the trespass of the one man [Adam]," that "through the disobedience of the one man the many were made sinners," and that "in Adam all die" (Psalms 51:5; 58:3; Romans 5:15, 19; 1 Corinthians 15:22).

We see such generational connectedness all the time. AIDS gets transferred from generation to generation. Child abusers beget child abusers, and alcoholics raise alcoholics. I couldn't have become an insulin-dependent diabetic without a genetic proclivity. Does the condition of my ancestors affect my life? Of course.

If we see such obvious physical connections to our ancestors, why not spiritual connections? Why shouldn't we see sin itself as a communicable disease, one passed on from parents to children? A good God, concerned for our welfare, must no more ignore our sin problem than a good physician would ignore a patient's disease.

This idea of inherited sin may seem unfair, but God is the proper judge of fairness. Learning to see our sin from his perspective is the first step toward finding freedom from it.

So long as we view evil as coming from sources *outside* us, we can view ourselves as victims, not perpetrators. When we sin, we imagine it's only because something or someone *made* us do so. But as it's been said, the truth isn't primarily that we're sinners because we sin; rather, we sin because we're sinners.

Although we've inherited sin, each of us is a sinner in his own right, and we'll all be judged for our own lifetime of sins. God "will render to each person according to his deeds" (Romans 2:6, NASB)—not according to Adam's deeds. Yes, we sinned in Adam, but God will judge us for our own sins (which will be plenty). "For he who does wrong will receive the consequences of the wrong which he has done, and that without partiality" (Colossians 3:25, NASB).

PROUD ILLUSION

This sin nature we've inherited means that apart from Christ, we differ only in degree—not in kind—from the most notorious murderer or most ruthless dictator.

Just fifteen miles from our home, Westley Allan Dodd tortured, molested, and murdered three boys in the late 1980s. Dodd was arrested, tried, and convicted for the crimes. Shortly after midnight on January 5, 1993, he was hanged.

Thirty minutes after he died, the twelve media eyewitnesses recounted the experience. I felt stunned as one of them read Dodd's last words: "I had thought there was no hope and no peace. I was wrong. I have found hope and peace in the Lord Jesus Christ."

Gasps and groans erupted from the gallery, fueled by palpable anger. The idea of God offering grace to Dodd utterly offended the crowd that had come to see justice done.

That's when it hit me in a deep and personal way—*I* am part of the same human race. I'd imagined the distance between Dodd and me as the difference between the South and North Poles. But from God's viewpoint, the distance is negligible. Apart from Christ, I am Dodd. I am Osama bin Laden. I am Hitler, Stalin, Mao. Only by the virtue of Christ can I stand forgiven before a holy God.

This isn't hyperbole; it's biblical truth. We'll never appreciate Christ's grace so long as we hold on to the proud illusion that we're better than we are. We flatter ourselves when we look at evil acts and say, "I would never do that." Given our evil natures and similar backgrounds, resources, and opportunities, we likely would.

But the greater our grasp of our sin and alienation from God, the greater our grasp of God's grace. Charles Spurgeon put it this way: "Too many think lightly of sin, and therefore think lightly of the Saviour."

We try to explain away sin in terms of "That's not what I meant" or "I did what my father always did to me" or "I wouldn't have done this if you hadn't done that." All these statements *minimize our evil and thereby minimize the greatness of God's grace in atoning for our evil.*

✳ Grace isn't about God lowering his standards. It's about God fulfilling those standards through the substitutionary suffering of Jesus Christ. Grace never ignores or violates truth. Grace gave what truth demanded: the ultimate sacrifice for our wickedness.

Taking Responsibility

Our culture continually reinforces the habit of denying responsibility and casting blame, which ultimately only intensifies evil and suffering. Exemplified by frivolous lawsuits, our culture of blame goes hand in hand with a sense of entitlement. We think we deserve the best and are offended when we don't get it.

We need to recover the lost art of blaming ourselves for what happens to us—especially as we tackle the problem of evil and suffering.

The London *Times* once asked various writers for essays on the topic "What's Wrong with the World?" G. K. Chesterton's contribution was perhaps the shortest essay in history.

> Dear Sirs:
>   I am.
>   Sincerely yours,
>   G. K. Chesterton

Daniel, a righteous man, came before God confessing the sins of his nation, not saying, "They have sinned," but, "*We* have sinned" (Daniel 9:5). He took full ownership for his own contribution to the problem of his nation's sin.

So should we all.

Notes

1. Jonathan Aitken, *John Newton: From Disgrace to Amazing Grace* (Wheaton, IL: Crossway Books, 2007), 347.
2. D. A. Carson, *The Difficult Doctrine of the Love of God* (Wheaton, IL: Crossway Books, 2000), 42.

3

Alternative Answers

*Examining Explanations
for Evil and Suffering*

Obviously, not everyone accepts the biblical viewpoint on evil and suffering. So what other explanations have been proposed? Let's explore the most prominent alternatives.

IMAGINARY EVIL

One proposed solution is to say, *"There is no evil and suffering."*

Buddhism sees suffering as nothing more than the gap between what I have and what I want. To get rid of suffering you get rid of all desire (including the desire to be free of pain). Nirvana, the end of suffering, is the extinction of all desire. Peter Kreeft points out that this is like killing the patient in order to cure the disease.[1]

Pantheists believe that *everything* is god; god is nature and nature is god. The things we call "evil" are therefore only imperfections in our view of reality that progressive self-realization and self-improvement can remove. They dismiss evil and suffering as unreal, an illusion. Well, if it's an illusion, it is certainly a painful one, isn't it?

In the face of so much obvious suffering in this world, it's surprising that many people hold this view.

IMAGINARY GOD

Another response is to say, *"There is no God."* Atheism has become more prominent in recent years, and its most common argument is the problem of suffering and evil.

One contemporary atheist expressed it this way: "None can account for the tremendous amount of suffering in a world in which an allegedly omnipotent, omniscient and wholly good God reigns."[2]

Her conclusion echoes that of many philosophers who see belief in God—at least in the Christian God who is good and caring and personal—as irrational.

In theory, the atheist could argue that the problem of evil is simply an internal inconsistency within Christianity. Without agreeing that true evils exist in the world, she could still say that the Christian belief in evil is inconsistent with belief in a good God.

I've read many atheists, however, and this is *not* typically what they argue. Instead, they present long lists of what *they* call evil—thus trying to hold God accountable to moral standards that can exist *only if there is a God.*

LIMITED DIVINE POWER

After Rabbi Harold Kushner's only son died in his teens from a rare disease, he wrote *When Bad Things Happen to Good People.* Some things are "too difficult even for God," Kushner said. "I can worship a God who hates suffering but cannot eliminate it, more easily than I can worship a God who chooses to make children suffer and die, for whatever exalted reason."[3] Kushner's book, published three decades ago, sold over four million copies and continues to influence many today.

Our culture's eroded view of God prepared the way for the book's staggering success. People welcomed a kindhearted God who *would* stop anything bad from happening to us…*if only he could.*

That view is echoed by the influential twentieth-century school of thought known as *process theology,* which conceives of God as always evolving. God supposedly emerges and grows with the universe. He is powerful but not all-powerful. Think of him as a conductor limited by an orchestra's skills. He can lead, but he can't control.

A limit on God's power is also implied in various dualistic views of God. If more than one god exists, then divine power is divided and cannot reside in a single God. Subtle forms of such dualism exist even among Christians, in how they view Satan in relation to God. Some believe that though God may win in the end, Satan has so much power and brings so much suffering and evil that God simply cannot stop him, at least for now.

Some see dualism as a single impersonal force, such as the Force in the *Star Wars* movies, with its light and dark sides. The winning side is always in doubt.

While these approaches may seem to provide a tidy resolution to the problem of evil, they utterly contradict Scripture. The Bible emphatically reveals God as all powerful, as in these verses from the prophet Isaiah: "I am God, and there is no other; I am God, and there is none like me…. I say: My purpose will stand, and I will do all that I please…. What I have said, that will I bring about; what I have planned, that will I do" (46:9–11).

A God who has high aspirations but only limited power to bring them about resembles our mothers. We love them for loving us and wanting our best, but those nice intentions go only so far in a world they can't control.

LIMITED DIVINE KNOWLEDGE

Some theologians believe that much of the future remains opaque to
God, and on that basis they argue that he is more loving and bears
less responsibility for the world's evil and suffering.

In the past twenty years, these "open theists" have asserted that
God does not and cannot know in advance the future choices
human beings will make. They suggest that a loving God took a calculated risk when he created mankind, and had he foreknown the
horrible things that would occur in human history, he might never
have created this world as he did. They believe this effectively dis-
tances God from evil human choices and the consequent suffering
they bring.

This view of God's limited knowledge conflicts with the Bible,
which insists throughout that God knows absolutely everything. King
David says, "O LORD, you have searched me and known me! You
know when I sit down and when I rise up; you discern my thoughts
from afar.… *Even before a word is on my tongue,* behold, O LORD, you
know it altogether" (Psalm 139:1–2, 4, ESV). David goes on to indi-
cate how God knew—from eternity past—everything that will happen each day of our lives: "Your eyes saw my unformed substance; in
your book were written, every one of them, the days that were formed
for me, when as yet there was none of them" (verse 16, ESV).

God is *"perfect in knowledge"* (Job 37:16). He *"knows everything"*
(1 John 3:20). "He determines the number of the stars and calls them
each by name" (Psalm 147:4). That's countless trillions of stars, each
named by God.

The Creator says, "I am God, and there is none like me. I make
known the end from the beginning, from ancient times, what is still
to come. I say: My purpose will stand, and I will do all that I please"

(Isaiah 46:9–10). How can God make known the end from the beginning? Only by *knowing* the end from the beginning.

When God said through the prophets that the Messiah would be born in Bethlehem and be crucified between two evildoers, he was not speculating but stating what he has always known. When he prophesied that Judas would betray Jesus for thirty pieces of silver and throw the money back to the priests, he knew exactly what choices people would make (see Zechariah 11:13; compare Matthew 27:3–7).

God even revealed to Elisha *what would have happened* if King Jehoash had struck the ground five or six times with arrows (see 2 Kings 13:19). Jesus said to some unbelievers, "If the miracles that were performed in you had been performed in Tyre and Sidon, they *would have* repented long ago" (Matthew 11:21).

Jesus told Peter that before a rooster crowed at a specific place and time, Peter would deny him not just twice, not four times, but *three* times (see John 13:38). This demonstrates detailed knowledge of the future.

Earlier, Jesus had said, "Simon, Simon, behold, Satan demanded to have you, that he might sift you like wheat, but I have prayed for you that your faith may not fail. And *when* you have turned again, strengthen your brothers" (Luke 22:31–32, ESV).

Notice that Jesus knew Peter's future choices, both that he would turn away from him *and* turn back to him. If he knew those details about Peter's future choices—not only denials and repentance, but the number of denials and the place and time down to when a particular rooster would crow—surely he knows the details about the future choices of all his creatures, including Satan, demons, and all people, unbelievers and believers alike.

We can be taken by surprise, but God cannot. This should encourage us. I find it easier to trust a God who has known about a tragedy all along—and planned in advance how he'll use it for his glory and for our good—than one who only just found out about it. We might compare the God of the Bible to a gifted surgeon who has studied a patient's case in advance and has planned a specific procedure to accomplish a particular purpose. He operates with a detailed foreknowledge of his patient's condition.

The God of open theism is more like an emergency room physician, also highly knowledgeable and skilled, but because he doesn't know his patient's condition when that patient gets wheeled in the door, the doctor must improvise—sometimes successfully, sometimes not.

Any surgeon will testify that surgeries planned and prepared for in advance have a higher success rate than emergency surgeries done on the fly. Which scenario would give you greater comfort?

I don't believe in picking fights about secondary doctrinal issues. But I'm convinced there's a great deal at stake in this issue of open theism, as it attempts to redefine the very nature of God. Fortunately, God will always remain who he is. The question is, as we try to modify him to resolve our intellectual struggles, what will become of us?

God doesn't need us to rescue him from the problem of evil, and particularly not at the cost of denying what the Bible so clearly affirms about him.

LIMITED DIVINE GOODNESS

Second-century Gnostics thought the world's evil proceeded from God's own being. Hence, they had no "problem of evil."

Centuries later, in *Thus Spake Zarathustra,* the highly influential philosopher Friedrich Nietzsche portrayed God as the creator of both good and evil—the source not only of truth, but also of lies.

Richard Dawkins, author of the bestseller *The God Delusion,* says it's as easy to imagine an evil God as a good one. In fact, he considers the God of the Old Testament an evil deity. Less extremely, a noted contemporary religion professor has written, "I affirm that God is good, but not perfectly good."[4] Is he right?

Again, the answer from the Bible is a clear no. Scripture insists— repeatedly and without qualification—that "the LORD is good" (see, for example, Psalms 25:8; 34:8; 119:68; and Nahum 1:7).

God is the greatest good as well as the source of all lesser goods: "Every good and perfect gift is from above, coming down from the Father" (James 1:17). As theologian Wayne Grudem expresses it, "The goodness of God means that God is the final standard of good, and that all that God is and does is worthy of approval."[5]

We lose sight of this when we define goodness from our own finite and fallen perspective, then criticize God for failing to fit our definition.

But to say that God is good is *not* to say God will always *appear* to be good, or that we'll always like him for being good. In reality, when suffering causes us to question God's goodness, it's because our own standard of goodness falls so far short of his. And God's goodness entails far more than whatever makes us feel comfortable and happy for the time being.

LIMITED DIVINE LOVE

Few critics argue philosophically that God lacks love. But many people start to doubt God's care when terrible things happen to them.

Often it's because we define love in superficial and trivial ways, setting us up to question God's love in hard times. But the Bible speaks repeatedly of God's *"unfailing* love" or *"steadfast* love" (as in Psalms 32:10 and 51:1, and Lamentations 3:32, NIV and ESV). God's constant love for us will never let us down, no matter how things appear.

When we define God's love as we please, then use that redefinition to neutralize other attributes of God that we find less appealing, we mirror our culture which values love but devalues holiness. Elevating God's love above his other character traits can breed resentment, anger, confusion, and disappointment when he allows us to suffer.

As he wrestled with the problem of evil after a terrible accident, a friend of mine said that he came to believe there's a fault in the logic of the major premise of the problem of evil. He said to me, "It shouldn't be limited to only two attributes of God—being loving and powerful—but it should include *all* of them—merciful, faithful, wise, holy, patient, glorious, etc."

My friend was right. While we still cannot understand all God's purposes, it's easier if we don't lock ourselves in to focusing on only two or three of his attributes. That God would demonstrate his holiness and glory through evil and suffering is just as legitimate and God-like as that he would demonstrate his love through his common grace and sending his Son. Anytime we limit his character to one, two, or three of our favorite attributes, we will not see the full picture of who he is, and we will therefore not be thinking of the true God, only a god of our imagination.

If love outweighs holiness, why not dispense altogether with Christ's crucifixion—especially since Jesus asked for this very thing, were it possible (as we see in Matthew 26:39)? The truth is, God's holiness and love combined at the cross of Christ; they constitute the only way possible to save sinners and still satisfy God's perfect nature.

Inadequate Worldview

In countering these various proposed solutions, we can summarize the Bible's perspective in this way: God is all-good, all-powerful, and all-knowing; he hates evil and will ultimately judge evildoers, and remove evil and suffering after accomplishing a greater, eternal good.

The Bible confirms evil's existence and considers all of God's attributes as infinite. Evil is never good, yet God can use any evil to accomplish good and sovereign purposes.

Everyone has a worldview—inconsistent and superficial though it might be. And I believe the greatest test of any worldview is how it deals with the problem of evil and suffering. I'm convinced that Christianity's explanatory power concerning evil and suffering beats that of any other worldview. It accounts for how this world came to be, and it offers the greatest hope for the world's future. It tells us why we can expect God to deliver his redeemed people forever from evil and suffering.

Many people who profess the alternative explanations mentioned above are indignant about evil—yet they reject a belief in God that's the only rational basis on which to define evil.

Notes

1. Peter Kreeft, *The Journey* (Downers Grove, IL: InterVarsity, 1996), 64.
2. Andrea M. Weisberger, *Suffering Belief* (New York: Peter Lang, 1999), 234.
3. Harold S. Kushner, *When Bad Things Happen to Good People* (New York: Schocken Books, 1981), 134.
4. John K. Roth, "A Theodicy of Protest," in *Encountering Evil*, ed.

Stephen T. Davis (Louisville, KY: Westminster John Knox, 2001), 31–32.

5. Wayne Grudem, *Systematic Theology* (Grand Rapids, MI: Zondervan, 1994), 197.

4

A Clash of Worldviews

*Investigating Relativism, Atheism,
and the "Problem" of Goodness*

How does your own worldview stack up against the real world around you? Does it credibly explain the way things are and offer persuasive reasons for believing in a hopeful future? Or do you need to revise or abandon it in order to embrace the biblical worldview?

OBJECTIVE STANDARDS

The account of evil and suffering in the Christian worldview is uniquely and profoundly God centered. It affirms that God's character provides the only objective standard for determining good and evil. This view is rooted in the words of God himself: "Be holy because I, the LORD your God, am holy" (Leviticus 19:2).

We would all agree that murderers and rapists have committed evil; we know they've defied moral standards and violated human rights. But *how* do we know this? We have a general consensus about many moral standards, but if God doesn't exist, on what objective basis could moral standards and human rights exist?

DOES EVERYONE HAVE THIS MORAL COMPASS

Moral relativists even insist that there's no such thing as a moral absolute—yet they fail to live within their own system. Just ask them to answer honestly this question: "If I beat you over the head with a baseball bat, raped your sister, kidnapped and tortured your child, and set fire to your house—would you consider any of those actions to be absolutely wrong?" Of course they would.

Ethical norms are not *invented* by humans, they are merely *discovered* by us. They predate us, going back to a source far more ancient and authoritative than ourselves. They go back to our Creator. If the majority believes it is right to own slaves, terminate unborn children, "put to sleep" the elderly, and evict the poor from housing, then the majority may rule, but they do not determine ethical standards—they simply violate them. God says of unbelievers, "They show that the requirements of the law are written on their hearts, their consciences also bearing witness, and their thoughts now accusing, now even defending them" (Romans 2:15). Despite arguments to the contrary, all of us, whether atheists or agnostics or Christians, believe in some moral absolutes. Who or what is behind those standards? Our truest conception of good is written on our hearts by God and comes from our having been created in his image. That doesn't mean our standards are consistently perfect, because unlike God we're finite in our understanding. What's worse, we each have a sin nature, one that's reinforced by our being surrounded by other people with sinful natures.

I've talked with individuals whose ethics have evolved over time, and who now believe that any consensual sex between adults is moral. Adultery is consensual sex, so is it moral? Well, yes, some would say, as long as the two partners genuinely love each other. But how moral is it in the eyes of the betrayed spouse? Or the children whose trust, hearts, and home are broken? Such hopeless subjectivity provides no moral framework at all.

The Bible, on the other hand, shows us a God who reveals himself through moral laws that reflect his character qualities, helping us see what God is like. The Bible offers an objective moral stance against adultery, for example, because marital infidelity violates God's characteristic of faithfulness; therefore, adultery is specifically forbidden in his Word. That's how we can know adultery is evil without depending on our moods and feelings. Our subjective preferences might whisper that adultery's okay, but God tells us in Scripture that it is dead wrong. End of discussion.

Even those who reject the claims of the Christian worldview should acknowledge that it does in fact offer a moral foundation for discerning good and evil. And they should ask themselves whether, without realizing it, they sometimes borrow from the Christian worldview because their own worldview cannot provide a foundation on which to judge good and evil. IS IT A CHRISTIAN WORLD VIEW OR A BIBLICAL WORLD VIEW?

The "Problem" of Goodness

Meanwhile, if we explore the meaning of evil frankly and forthrightly, we can't miss another profound point that also argues for the Christian worldview and the existence of God.

Yes, this hurting world has truckloads of evil, but it also has boatloads of good. Where did it all come from? While atheists routinely speak of the problem of evil, they usually don't raise the problem of goodness. But if you argue that evil is evidence against God's existence, you must also admit that good is evidence for it. If a good God doesn't exist, what's the source of goodness?

The very act of calling evil a problem presupposes a standard of goodness. If God doesn't exist, by what objective basis can anyone measure morality?

For the atheist, there are no grounds for a solution to the problem of evil and suffering, or for higher expectations—only for wishful thinking. The atheists' argument that goodness and moral standards can exist without God doesn't hold up. In an evolutionary worldview, where the natural world is all there is, why object to stronger human beings stealing from or killing weaker ones? Wouldn't this simply be natural selection and survival of the fittest, not a question of right or wrong?

If there's no God, then people don't live after death and aren't held accountable for their actions, good or evil. That's why Dostoevsky said, "Destroy a man's belief in immortality and…everything would be permitted, even cannibalism."[1]

A naturalistic worldview based on evolution can explain greed, selfishness, insensitivity, survival preoccupation, and even a certain amount of ruthlessness; but how can it explain acting with kindness, putting other people first, and even risking one's life to help a stranger? Why does anyone feel gratitude? And why do people, even irreligious survivors of a plane crash, so often thank God? Do people thank time, chance, and natural selection for the good they experience? No, because innately we see life as a gift, and a gift requires a giver—in this case, God.

Why do people have such a strong sense of right and wrong? A system that operates on brute strength and genetic superiority can explain and justify racism, sexism, and oppression. But it cannot explain goodness, humility, compassion, and mercy. What should surprise atheists is not that powerful people sometimes crush those weaker than themselves, but that many powerful people make sacrifices to aid the weak. Why do they do it?

⟶ If naturalism were an accurate worldview, the ruthlessness seen in abortion should characterize our society at every level. And yet we have children's hospitals spending vast resources to help the terminally ill, we see Special Olympics for disabled children and adults, and we find special parking everywhere for handicapped people. These are all shocking aberrations from natural selection, which would normally welcome the death of the weak, the diseased, and the disabled.

The fact that we don't question good's existence affirms our basic instinct that good is the norm and evil the exception. Even the atheist who points out the horrors of evil is testifying to good as the norm. Unwittingly, her moral objection to evil and suffering is an argument for a good God.

Moreover, the sacrificial good done by many Christians in the face of evil also testifies to God's existence. Atheists often emphasize the evils done in religion's name, but they say virtually nothing about how modern education, science, and health care all emerged out of Christianity. Compare the Red Cross, an organization that has done incalculable good for millions across the world, to the much publicized witch hunts of old New England, in which a total of nineteen people died, or even to the Inquisition, responsible for an average of five deaths a year in its four-hundred-fifty-year history.[2]

While some professing Christians have certainly perpetrated injustice in the name of Christ, the numbers pale in comparison to the multimillions slaughtered by the eager disciples of atheists such as Nietzsche and Lenin—including Hitler, Stalin, and Mao.

In summary, we can assert here again the Christian worldview that although evil is never good, God can use any evil to accomplish his good and sovereign purposes. As Joni Eareckson Tada writes, "God permits what he hates to accomplish that which he loves."[3] We see that truth most profoundly in what happened to Jesus on the cross.

Notes

1. Fyodor Dostoevsky, *The Brothers Karamazov* (New York: Random House, 1970), 88.
2. My thanks to Dinesh D'Souza for making this point while speaking at our church in October 2008.
3. Joni Eareckson Tada, *Pearls of Great Price: 366 Daily Devotional Readings* (Grand Rapids, MI: Zondervan, 2006), 387.

5

The Great Drama

*Reviewing the Roles of Evil
and Suffering in Christ's Redemptive Work*

THE FALL SET OFF A SERIES OF EVENTS THAT ARE
STILL IN PROGRESS TODAY

REMOVES THE REASON
FOR JUSTIFICATION

Because the Fall had really happened in history, God's Son had to enter history (incarnation), suffer and die in history (redemption), and rise from the grave in history (resurrection).

Romans 5:12–21 assumes that a real Adam and Eve fell in history. Other passages affirm the same (see 1 Corinthians 15:22, 45; 1 Timothy 2:13–14). Paul speaks of Adam as the historical head of humanity in the same way that he speaks of Christ as the new head of redeemed humanity. Adam was no more fictional than Jesus. I HAVE NEVER QUESTIONED THE REALITY OF JESUS

In *Genesis in Space and Time,* Francis Schaeffer stressed the importance of not fictionalizing the events of the early chapters of Genesis. Whenever these events are reduced to folk tales, ultimately the gospel gets reduced to fables. If Adam and Eve were not real people and therefore never chose to commit evil, then Christ's redemptive work can also be seen as symbolic rather than historical.

Adam and Eve's story is real—but try responding to it in a fresh way by reflecting on this question: if you, instead of God, were the author of this story…how would *you* have written it?

UNFOLDING NARRATIVE

Think of God as the Great Storyteller. With grand artistry, he brings forth a beautiful world in a spectacular universe (as we see in Genesis, the Bible's first book). As the culmination of his creativity, he fashions Adam and Eve. He could have shielded them from Satan's temptations, warding off evil and suffering and humanity's curse. But he did not. As a result, the man and woman rebel against God, and evil enters the world.

Thousands of years go by as humanity's struggle only intensifies. God promises a Redeemer, and with eagerness his people look for one to come forth triumphantly, overthrowing their enemies and setting up his kingdom. But the centuries continue to pass without the Redeemer's appearance.

Finally, in a fantastic plot twist, God becomes a humble carpenter, heals the sick, raises the dead, and allows his enemies to kill him. He does it all to redeem the people he loves. He rises from the dead, commands and empowers his followers to serve him, then leaves but promises to return. With the force of his own resurrection to back it up, he reiterates the promise: one day he'll make all things right and will come to live forever with his people.

The first three chapters of God's story set up this unfolding drama of redemption. The Bible's last three chapters show how God will judge evil, reward good, and come down to the New Earth to live with his children forever. He'll wipe away every tear from their eyes, and there'll be no more suffering and evil.

It's the greatest story ever told, and the prototype of all great stories.

But suppose *you* are its author. Not liking that miserable part about Satan's temptation and Adam and Eve's sin, you strike it out.

You also eliminate the ensuing conflicts, hatreds, lies, and murders that have marked one century after another. You erase all wars and heartbreaks, all yearnings for something better. Take them all away...but *you would also take away Jesus.* There would be no God-man, no incarnation, no *need* for incarnation. No first coming, no second coming. No New Heaven and New Earth, only the same one continuing forever.

As with all narratives, *without conflict, there is no story.* Without the huge problem, there can be no wondrous solution. Without the high stakes of humanity's alienation from God, there can be no redemption.

Erasing the struggle and suffering from this story would mean less appreciation for peace because war had never broken out; less appreciation for food because famine had never occurred; less appreciation for righteousness because sin never appeared; less love for life because death never happened; and less glory to God and heartfelt worship because we'd never have seen his attributes of grace and mercy and patience.

It's understandable to wish for a world untouched by evil and suffering. But which version of the story is more satisfying? Which would you prefer to watch unfold?

DRAMATIC RESOLUTION

Jesus Christ's life and death demonstrate that God has never dished out any suffering he hasn't taken on himself.

His death on the cross is God's answer to the question, "Why don't you do something about evil?" God allowed Jesus' temporary suffering so he could prevent our eternal suffering.

In the Old Testament, we read how God kept reaching down to his people. "The LORD...sent word to them through his messengers again and again, because he had pity on his people.... But they mocked God's messengers, despised his words and scoffed at his prophets" (2 Chronicles 36:15–16).

Finally God sent his Son to Earth. He came in humiliation; many imagined him conceived out of wedlock, a shameful thing in that era. He grew up in a town of ill repute: "Nazareth! Can anything good come from there?" (John 1:46).

He worked as a humble carpenter, lived in relative poverty, and endured many indignities as he spent three years in a ministry teaching and healing and speaking the good news of God's kingdom.

God wrote the script of this drama of redemption long before Satan, demons, Adam and Eve—and you and I—took the stage. And from the beginning, he knew that the utterly spectacular ending would make the dark middle worth it. Paul writes, "This grace was given us in Christ Jesus *before the beginning of time*" (2 Timothy 1:9). How could God give us grace before our lives began, even before the universe itself existed? Only because God knew and determined in advance the work of Christ for us on the Cross.

The story's low point is the death of Jesus, yet this low point is the basis upon which he will one day, in a dramatic resolution to the story, return to establish his eternal kingdom on Earth.

BREATHTAKING TRUTH

When I read God's story as a curious teenage unbeliever—having been raised with no knowledge of God—part of what drew me to Christ is how the gospel accounts seem so contrary to typical human reasoning, yet I found them completely credible. No human would make up such a story! To me it had the ring of truth…and still has.

If the gospel story is well known to us, sometimes that very familiarity prevents us from understanding its breathtaking nature. That's one benefit of reading other redemptive stories that give us glimpses of the greatest one. To me, *The Lion, the Witch and the Wardrobe* offers particular help in understanding Christ's atoning sacrifice.

Aslan, the all-powerful lion, created Narnia and all worlds. After Lucy hears that her brother must die for his treachery, she asks Aslan, "Can anything be done to save Edmund?"

"All shall be done," Aslan responds. "But it may be harder than you think." In fact, he can save Edmund only through his self-sacrifice. Knowing the terrible suffering and death that await him, Aslan becomes very sad.

Aslan's foe, the White Witch, commands her servants to roll Aslan onto his back and tie his paws together. "Had the Lion chosen," the story says, "one of those paws could have been the death of them all." Finally, the witch orders them to shave Aslan. They cut off his beautiful mane and ridicule him. Aslan, their rightful king, surrenders to his enemies, trading his life for Edmund's.[1]

Likewise, Jesus felt overwhelming sadness in the Garden of Gethsemane. He told his disciples, "My soul is crushed with grief to the point of death. Stay here and keep watch with me" (Matthew 26:38, NLT). The soldiers who guarded Jesus mocked him and hit him. Then Jesus went to the cross to die for us.

That's how much he loves us. And that's why seeking answers for the problem of evil and suffering should turn us toward Jesus in a fresh way.

S.M. ROE

LAST WORD

Someone told me the story of a teenager who didn't want to be seen in public with her mother because her mother's arms were terribly disfigured. One day when her mother took her shopping and reached out her hand, a clerk looked horrified. Later, crying, the girl told her mother how embarrassed she was.

Understandably hurt, the mother waited an hour before going to her daughter's room to tell her, for the first time, what had happened.

"When you were a baby, I woke up to a burning house. Your room was an inferno. Flames were everywhere. I could have gotten out the front door, but I decided I'd rather die with you than leave you to die alone. I ran through the fire and wrapped my arms around you. Then I went back through the flames, my arms on fire. When I got outside on the lawn, the pain was agonizing, but when I looked at you, all I could do was rejoice that the flames hadn't touched you."

Stunned, the girl looked at her mother through new eyes. Weeping in shame and gratitude, she kissed her mother's marred hands and arms.

God doesn't merely empathize with our sufferings. He actually suffers. Jesus is God; what he suffered, God suffered. God paid the highest price on our behalf; we therefore have no grounds for believing he doesn't "get it." The drama of evil and suffering in Christ's sacrifice addresses the very heart of the problem of evil and suffering. And one day it will prove to have been the final answer.

Whenever you feel tempted in your suffering to ask God, "Why are you doing this *to* me?" look at the Cross and ask, "Why did you do that *for* me?"

There was a time when I could not fully accept any explanation that didn't make sense to me, start to finish. However, I've come to trust my own understanding less, and God's Word more. I find a strange delight in being swallowed up by the immensity of God's greatness and by the divine mysteries that once disturbed me. Knowing that I'll sit before God's judgment seat—not he before mine—I choose to trust him. And the more I do, the more sense the story makes to me.

And I am certain about this: the best answer to the problem of evil is a person—Jesus Christ. I'm convinced he is the *only* answer.

In this world of suffering and evil, I have a profound and abiding hope, and faith for the future—not because I follow a set of religious rules to make me better, but because for forty years I've known a real person, and today I know him better than ever. Through inconceivable self-sacrifice he has touched me deeply, given me a new heart, and utterly transformed my life.

Because Jesus willingly entered this world of evil and suffering and didn't spare himself, but took on the worst of it for my sake and yours, he has earned my trust even for what I can't understand. Just like countless others, many of whom have suffered profoundly, I've found him to be trustworthy.

When it comes to goodness and evil, present suffering and eternal joy...the first Word, and the last, is *Jesus*.

Last Day

The future will fully vindicate God's righteous integrity and the wisdom of the story as he has written it, because of what he has done in Jesus.

As God culminates his plan of the ages, Heaven's inhabitants will cry out, "Great and marvelous are your deeds, Lord God Almighty. Just and true are your ways, King of the ages. Who will not fear you, O Lord, and bring glory to your name? For you alone are holy. All nations will come and worship before you, for your righteous acts have been revealed" (Revelation 15:3–4).

That God's righteous acts will be revealed, that his ways will be shown as just and true, means that God *will* vindicate his character. When he does, and when eternal judgment falls upon those who refuse to repent, no clear-thinking being will ever again view evil and suffering as evidence against God's existence, omnipotence, omniscience, goodness, or love. When we see God for who he is, we'll credit him with all goodness and will blame him for no evil.

As we kneel in his presence, the "problem of evil and suffering" will vanish like a shadow under the noonday sun.

Note

1. C. S. Lewis, *The Lion, the Witch and the Wardrobe* (New York: HarperCollins, 1978), 151–55.

6

Why So Much Evil?

Questioning Why God Allows Evil
and Delays Justice

WE MUST NOT BE LEARNING

Now that Jesus has triumphed over sin and death in his cross and resurrection, why does our world *still* contain so much evil and suffering?

Why did Jesus suffer the relentless beatings, then hang on the cross for six hours rather than six seconds or six minutes? Perhaps part of the answer is to remind us that suffering is a process. God doesn't end our suffering as soon as we would like. Nor did he end his Son's suffering as soon as he would have liked. We stand in good company.

Another part of the answer is simply that there's more God intends to accomplish in humanity and in each of our individual lives in this world. In his love and wisdom, suffering is sometimes the best means to complete this work, for his glory.

PAINFUL PROGRESS

This process by which we mature is built into our God-given humanity. If we have faith in Christ, then God has declared us to be righteous through his death, but God also wants us to *become* righteous. It may sound good to somehow skip the growing process of living under the Curse in this world, and to immediately get ushered into eternity without facing suffering. But that wouldn't accomplish God's highest purpose for us.

Someday this Earth will be remade into a new world. Meanwhile, God is not only preparing a place for us, he's preparing *us* for that place, through our suffering and growth in character.

C. S. Lewis, in *The Problem of Pain,* touches on the love that lies behind this process:

> To the puppy the whole proceeding [being washed, house trained, and disciplined] would seem, if it were a theologian, to cast grave doubts on the "goodness" of man: but the full-grown and full-trained dog, larger, healthier, and longer-lived than the wild dog, and admitted, as it were by Grace, to the whole world of affections, loyalties, interests, and comforts entirely beyond its animal destiny, would have no such doubts....
>
> He [God] does not house-train the earwig or give baths to centipedes. We may wish, indeed, that we were of so little account to God that He left us alone over trying to train us into something so unlike our natural selves: but once again, we are asking not for more Love, but for less.[1]

God's redemptive plan was not an ad-lib response to unanticipated events. From before the very beginning, God knew the very worst. And the very best it would one day bring.

We prefer that God would immediately crush and remove evil, not allowing it to hurt us. And because we know God is all-powerful, we may be puzzled why he doesn't immediately demonstrate his power by preventing tragedies and healing diseases. But power isn't God's only attribute. He's also glorified in showing his wisdom, which is best seen over time. Someday—if not in this life, then later in eternity when we're fully in his presence—we'll marvel at his love and wisdom in not preventing certain evils that he used for our ultimate good, in ways we never could have imagined.

"GRATUITOUS" EVIL

The atheistic worldview simply cannot account for superhuman evil. Death, yes; suffering, yes. But calculated, relentless, exhausting brutality toward the weak and innocent? The death camps? The Nazi doctors? The Killing Fields? The despicable acts of apparently "normal" people?

Jesus gave us the answer for supernatural evil when he said of Satan, "He was a murderer from the beginning" (John 8:44).

I have a friend who heard a man describe seeing children in Sudan forced to hack their parents to death with machetes. The man said, "I now believe in God, for I have met the devil." Extreme evil can wake us up to the reality of both good and evil, testifying to the invisible realities of God and Satan.

Great evils such as rape and murder certainly *look* gratuitous. But are we qualified to say they really are? Didn't the terrible murders of five young missionaries in Ecuador in 1956 seem senseless? Yet in retrospect nearly every missionary in the world sees great and far-reaching good that came out of their deaths.

Unbelievers and believers both call certain things utterly evil, including child abuse. Some will cite such evil as evidence against God. But others will see things for what they are and come face to face with the supernatural. When evil grows terrible enough, the unbeliever may abandon the sinking ship of moral relativism and its conviction that absolute evil doesn't exist.

Because the Christian worldview offers a well-grounded explanation for both human and superhuman evil, and a solid basis for moral outrage, those who find themselves morally outraged owe themselves a careful look at it.

"POINTLESS" SUFFERING

Ever been to a football game at half time when the band forms words or pictures in the middle of the field? They look great from up in the stands. But what if you're on the sidelines when the band forms its symbols? You can't see them. What the band's doing appears pointless, confusing, apparently meaningless. We see life from the sidelines. God sees it from above, in the grandstands. The Bible invites us to trust God that one day, when we can see from Heaven's perspective, many things will make sense that don't appear to when we're on the sidelines.

Holocaust survivor Viktor Frankl said in *Man's Search for Meaning*, "There is nothing in the world…that would so effectively help one to survive even the worst conditions as the knowledge that there is meaning in one's life."[2] He added, "Despair is suffering without meaning." Frankl found meaning in his suffering and thereby avoided despair. His point was, *something can be tragic without being meaningless.*

To label suffering as pointless, we must be able to see clearly that it lacks any point—but we can't. Imagine an air traffic controller instructing a pilot to assume a certain altitude and to take a certain line of descent. The pilot might argue, "That doesn't make sense to me. It would be easier to make a different approach." But he doesn't argue because he knows hundreds of other flights come in and out each hour. Good pilots must know the limits of their understanding and trust those who have the big picture, who can see the potential consequences of each pilot's decisions. Romans 8:28

What if knowing God and growing in faith and becoming more Christlike *is* the point of my existence? What if the universe is not about human comfort and happiness?

If we could stop it, we wouldn't allow a child to be born with a severe disability. But what if, without that child's disability, the parents would become self-absorbed rather than servant-hearted people, and their marriage would end in a bitter divorce? What if the disability influenced the child in such a way to cause him to come to faith in Christ, to grow up loving God, and then to spend eternity with his Savior and also with his parents? Since we're not God, we can't know.

Behind almost every human expression of the problem of evil stands the assumption that somehow we know what God *should* do. But unlike him, we are not all-knowing, all-wise, all-loving, all-powerful, and perfectly good—so how *could* we know? As finite and fallen individuals, how can we presume to judge God? Compared to him, we know very little, and even that is often distorted. We simply lack the necessary qualifications to assess what God should or shouldn't do.

HUMAN FREEDOM

To argue that God shouldn't permit evil or suffering is to argue against not only human choice, but love.

Can real love exist without freedom? I want my wife to love me simply because she wants to. I may inspire or win her love through my devotion to her, but I cannot dictate it, nor would I if I could. Forced love is no love at all. Love requires the freedom *not* to love. Meaningful choice must exist for love to exist.

But couldn't God eliminate at least the very worst forms of evil and suffering?

We might think a good and all-powerful God should disarm every shooter and prevent every drunk driver from crashing. But if God did that, this would not be a real world in which people make consequential choices. It would not be a world of character development and faith building. It would not be a world where family members put their arms around one another to face life's difficulties together. It would be a world where people went blithely along in life, happy to do evil as well as put up with evil, feeling no incentive to turn to God or to consider the gospel or to prepare for eternity. They would live with no sense of need—and then die, only to find themselves in Hell.

Peter van Inwagen writes, "If God simply 'canceled' all the horrors of this world by an endless series of miracles, he would thereby frustrate his own plan of reconciliation. If he did that, we should be content with our lot and should see no reason to cooperate with him."[3]

Ironically, those who most value the freedom to choose are quickest to condemn God for allowing evil and suffering.

Critics of a God who allows evil and suffering may feel deeply that they should have the freedom to smoke, or drive at the speed they wish, or not to wear seat belts or bicycle helmets. Then when they get injured or inflict injury on others, they question God's goodness, unwilling to take responsibility for the consequences of the choices they so value.

Freedom to do good, which can bring enjoyable consequences, cannot exist without the corresponding freedom to do evil, which brings suffering.

We can't influence each other for good unless we can also influence each other for evil. If I could not hurt you, I could not help you. If you could not kill me, you could not die for me.

God made the world as he did so that we could live in relationships where our choices have consequences in the lives of others. If we value freedom, we value a world that allows both good and evil choices. If we say we wish God made humans without the freedom to do evil, we are saying we don't think humans should have freedom. Which is to say that humans shouldn't be human.

The reality of evil and suffering in this world points to a God who despises evil but values freedom. He desires meaningful relationships with his creatures—and that requires a degree of freedom on our part.

CHANGED PERSPECTIVE

Experiences like those of missionaries David and Svea Flood lead many to conclude that even noble sacrifices can have pointless endings.

In the early twentieth century, the Floods left Sweden and made great sacrifices to serve God in the Belgian Congo. They and another young couple, the Ericksons, felt God's leading to take the gospel to a remote area called N'dolera.

Because a tribal chief would not let them enter his village, they had contact only with a young boy who sold them food. This boy was led to Jesus by Svea Flood. Then malaria struck, and the Ericksons returned to the central mission station, while the Floods remained alone near N'dolera. Svea died shortly after giving birth to a girl.

Stunned and disillusioned, David dug a crude grave where he buried his young wife. He gave his baby girl, Aina, to the Ericksons and returned to Sweden embittered, saying God had ruined his life.

Soon thereafter, the Ericksons suddenly died. Aina again had no one to care for her.

Why did all this happen? What possible good could have come from such a string of tragedies?

I am about to tell you the rest of the story, but keep in mind that it unfolded over many years, and none of those aware of this heartbreaking story knew the eventual outcome—except God.

Eventually, American missionaries brought Aina to the United States where she was adopted, becoming Aggie Hurst. Years later, a Swedish Christian magazine appeared in Aggie's mailbox. She didn't understand the words, but a photo inside shocked her. It showed a grave with a white cross, marked with a name she recognized—that of her mother, Svea Flood.

A college professor translated the article for Aggie. It told of missionaries who came to N'dolera long ago, of a young mother who died when her baby was born, and of a little African boy whom the woman had led to Christ before she died. That boy grew up and built a school in his village. Gradually he won his students to Christ, and the children led their parents to Christ. Even the tribal chief became a Christian.

Stirred by this story, Aggie felt an urge to try to find her father, with whom she had lost all contact long before.

After decades of bitterness, one day an old and ill David Flood had a visitor. Aggie told her father the story recounted in the article. "Today," she said, "there are six hundred African people serving Christ because you and Mother were faithful to God's call in your life."

David felt stunned. His heart softened. Just weeks before he died, he turned back to God.

Aggie eventually met that African boy, who had grown up to become the superintendent of a national church in Zaire (formerly the Belgian Congo; now the Democratic Republic of the Congo), an association of 110,000 baptized believers.[4]

The great tragedies in the lives of David, Svea, and Aina Flood were undeniably heartbreaking. They appeared utterly cruel and pointless. But in time they yielded a great harvest of joy that will continue for eternity.

I'm convinced that no evil, even truly horrible evil, is completely pointless. I'm assured of that by God's goodness and sovereignty, and also by knowing that he has a purpose for the world as stated in passages like Ephesians 1:11, which speaks of "the plan of him who works out everything in conformity with the purpose of his will."

RESTRAINED EVIL

The chaos that breaks out in some corner of the world always proves the exception rather than the rule. Otherwise it wouldn't be the lead story on the news. Why haven't tyrants, with access to powerful weapons, destroyed this planet? What has kept infectious diseases and natural disasters from killing 99 percent of the world's population rather than less than 1 percent?

In the collapse of New York's Twin Towers, fifteen thousand people came out alive, five times more than those who died. While this doesn't remove the pain felt by grieving families, it shows that even on that terrible day, suffering was limited.

My wife, Nanci, once said to me, "Given the evil of the human heart, you'd think there would be thousands of Jack the Rippers in every city." Her statement stopped me in my tracks. Might God be limiting sin all around us all the time? If God permitted people to follow their every evil inclination all the time, life on this planet would screech to a halt.

Sometimes God permits evil by giving people over to their sins (see Romans 1:24–32), and this itself leads to the deterioration and ultimate death of an evil culture, which is a mercy to surrounding cultures. The most morally corrupt ancient cultures no longer exist.

"But many children suffer; why doesn't God protect them?" We don't know the answer, but we also don't know how often God does protect children. The concept of guardian angels seems to be suggested by various passages (see, for example, Matthew 18:10).

God gives us a brief, dramatic look into the unseen world in which righteous angels battle evil ones, intervening on behalf of God's people (see Daniel 10:12–13, 20). How many angels has God sent to preserve the lives of children and shield them from harm?

My earliest memory is of falling into deep water and nearly drowning; someone my family didn't know jumped in and rescued me. As a parent and a grandparent I have seen many close calls, where it appears a child should have died or suffered a terrible injury, but somehow escaped both.

I believe God is in fact restraining a great deal of evil in this world, and for this we should thank him daily.

This thought, of course, doesn't keep our hearts from breaking when someone we love suffers or dies. Still, though I can't prove it, I'm convinced God prevents far more evil than he allows. I also believe he actively restrains the tests and temptations that come our way so that we won't experience anything greater than we can bear.

1st COR 10:13

Measured Suffering

The fact is, no matter how much God reduced world suffering, we'd still think he did too little.

How much evil and suffering is too much? Could God reduce the amount without restricting meaningful human choice, or decreasing the urgency of the message that the world's gone desperately wrong and we need to turn to the Redeemer before we die?

Suppose we rated all pain on a scale of one to ten. Say "engulfed in flames" got a ten rating while "mild sunburn" received a one. If God eliminated level-ten pain, then level-nine pain would become the worst—the new level ten. God could reduce the worst suffering to level three, but then level three, now the worst, would seem unbearable.

Any argument that judges God's goodness strictly by his elimination of pain will, in the end, not leave us satisfied if he permits any pain at all.

Greater Good

Although this world may seem very far from the best it could possibly be, its present condition may indeed be the best means to achieve the best possible world. A world that had never been touched by evil *would* be a good place, but would it be the best place possible? If we acknowledge, for example, that evil and suffering often bring out significant human virtues, we must answer no.

If you tell God he should not have allowed evil and suffering into the world, you're also saying he shouldn't allow compassion, mercy, and sacrificial love—which are all responses to imperfection and suffering. God had to permit evil and suffering so that those characteristics could develop in us. Can we fault God for ordaining the kind of world in which we could experience such great good?

Consider also that such attributes as patience, mercy, love, and strength of character, once developed, can last forever—long after evil has disappeared. Could this justify God's allowance of evil? I believe the answer is yes.

Our sufferings will prove to be far less than the goodness that awaits us: "I consider that our present sufferings are not worth comparing with the glory that will be revealed in us" (Romans 8:18). But God tells us even more than that. He says our sufferings will actually contribute to the greater good that awaits us: "For our light and momentary troubles are achieving for us an eternal glory that far outweighs them all" (2 Corinthians 4:17). ALSO VS 16 & 18

Think about what those two verses promise. Meditate on them; memorize them; say them aloud as you ask God for grace and empowerment to make it through your hardest days.

Bigger Picture

God's is not a vending-machine justice in which a coin of righteousness immediately produces reward, or a coin of evil yields swift retribution. Packaged theologies seek to neatly account for everything, but as Job, Psalms, and the prophets repeatedly demonstrate, that's not how life works.

No evil will go forever unpunished. The wheels of justice may seem to turn slowly, but they turn surely. Scripture assures us that justice is coming: "God will bring every deed into judgment, including every hidden thing, whether it is good or evil" (Ecclesiastes 12:14). Justice is certain, even when it isn't immediate.

Since sin demands death (see Romans 6:23), if people are to live, justice must wait.

God delays justice not to make our lives miserable, but to make our lives possible.

Throughout history God has delayed justice, both upon believers and unbelievers, to give them time to come to him, grow in Christlikeness, and trust him more deeply.

Don't we give thanks for God's patience with Saul, the self-righteous killer who became Paul? Or John Newton, the evil slave trader who accepted God's amazing grace and preached and wrote the song that countless millions have sung? Are we grateful for God's patience with us? Think of those who endured many years of suffering before the day you came to faith in Christ. Aren't you thankful God did not deliver this planet from the Curse when millions asked for relief, before you heard the gospel? I came to Christ in 1969. What if Christ had returned and brought final judgment in 1968? Or in 1950, before I was born? If God had brought justice long ago, where would you and I be today? We would either not exist, or we would have been ushered into an eternity without Christ.

After the September 11, 2001, terrorist attacks, American politicians made sweeping promises: "We're going to rid the world of this evil!" *This* evil meant the evil that had hurt us. (And evil it surely was.) But we can't ask that the world be rid of evil without asking that the world be rid of *us*.

Like Zebedee's sons, we would love to call down fire from Heaven to judge others' evil (see Luke 9:52–56). But we're slow to see our own evil. We want selective justice, not true justice. We cry out for justice when we really want vindication and special treatment—relief from injustices done *against* us, without being judged for injustices done *by* us. Since God is just, *he cannot always give us the justice we want without also giving us the justice we deserve.*

In truth, God doesn't delay justice for as long as we often imagine. Sometimes the rewards for goodness and the punishments of evil are quickly apparent in this life. And though ultimate rewards and punishments await our final judgment, considerable justice—both reward and retribution—gets dispensed the moment we die. That's when God's children immediately experience the joy of his presence, while those who are unrepentant encounter the first justice of Hell. This means that the maximum duration of injustice experienced by any person cannot exceed his life span.

Human parents, with good reason, frequently delay justice for their children. If your son disobeys when seated in the back of the car, you may postpone discipline until you get off the freeway and arrive home. If he's older, you may deprive him of a future privilege, such as attending a concert or staying overnight at a friend's. Likewise, if your child does an exceptional job on her homework or accomplishes something noteworthy in academics or athletics, you might let her choose something special to do during summer vacation.

In a sense, the anticipation of future joy and privilege—or future loss—brings the future event to the present, making us joyful (or disappointed) now.

God delays justice for greater durations and on a larger scale, but it's the same principle. So if we can rightfully delay rewards and punishments, why shouldn't God?

Notes

1. C. S. Lewis, *The Problem of Pain* (New York: Macmillan, 1962), 43.
2. Viktor E. Frankl, *Man's Search for Meaning* (New York: Simon and Schuster, 1985), 126.

3. Peter van Inwagen, ed., *Christian Faith and the Problem of Evil* (Grand Rapids, MI: Eerdmans, 2004), 71.

4. Aggie Hurst, "A Story of Eternal Perspective," Eternal Perspective Ministries, www.epm.org/artman2/publish/missions_true_stories/ A_Story_of_Eternal_Perspective.shtml.

7

God's Control
and Our Freedom

*Discovering How God Rules
Despite Our Choices*

Aconference speaker instructed the audience to each fold a sheet of paper in half, then open it back up. On the top half, they were to write the worst things that had happened to them. On the bottom half, they were to write the best things.[1] Invariably, people doing this end up with some of the same things listed on both the top and bottom of the page.

Try making your own list. If you've lived long enough, if enough time has passed since some of those "worst things" happened to you, you'll almost certainly find an overlap. I sure did.

How is this possible?

Because God is both loving *and* sovereign. Our lists provide persuasive proof that while evil and suffering are not good, God can use them to accomplish immeasurable good. Knowing this should give us great confidence that even when we don't see any redemptive meaning in our suffering, *God* can see it—and one day we will too. We can trust that God has a purpose for whatever he does and whatever he permits.

Margaret Clarkson wrote,

> The sovereignty of God is the one impregnable rock to which
> the suffering human heart must cling. The circumstances sur-
> rounding our lives are no accident: they may be the work of
> evil, but that evil is held firmly within the mighty hand of
> our sovereign God.... All evil is subject to Him, and evil can-
> not touch His children unless He permits it. God is the Lord
> of human history and of the personal history of every mem-
> ber of His redeemed family.[2]

THANK YOU

SOVEREIGN CONTROL

To better understand how short-term evil and suffering sometimes
accomplishes long-term good, we need a clear picture of God's *sovereignty*. His sovereignty means that everything always stays under
God's rule; nothing happens without either his direction or permission. God's sovereignty gives him ownership and authority over the
entire universe.

Countless passages affirm God's sovereign control over human
lives and circumstances. "He does whatever he pleases," Job affirmed
(23:13). In prayer, David acknowledged, "You are the ruler of all
things" (1 Chronicles 29:12). The Babylonian ruler Nebuchadnezzar
was forced to affirm, "The Most High rules the kingdom of men"
(Daniel 4:17, ESV). And Paul praised God as "the blessed and only
Ruler, the King of kings and Lord of lords" (1 Timothy 6:15).

Even what appears random is not: "The lot is cast into the lap,
but its every decision is from the LORD" (Proverbs 16:33). If we
believe these verses, our reactions to many of the difficulties we face

will change. Problems will seem smaller; though we can't control them, we know God can.

FINITE FREEDOM

This doctrine of God's sovereignty inevitably enters the picture when we examine the problem of evil and suffering—and our state of mind determines whether this doctrine comforts us or threatens us.

In his nineteenth-century poem *Invictus,* William Ernest Henley captures the proud human spirit:

> It matters not how strait the gate,
> How charged with punishments the scroll,
> I am the master of my fate:
> I am the captain of my soul.

The proud human heart doesn't want to submit to almighty God. We want to make our own plans, do our own thing, and have it our way. James identifies the arrogance and evil boasting underlying our presumption that we can do whatever we wish without submitting to God's plan:

> Now listen, you who say, "Today or tomorrow we will go to this or that city, spend a year there, carry on business and make money." Why, you do not even know what will happen tomorrow. What is your life? You are a mist that appears for a little while and then vanishes. Instead, you ought to say, "If it is the Lord's will, we will live and do this or that." As it is, you boast and brag. All such boasting is evil. (4:13–16)

We delude ourselves when we think we have ultimate control over our lives. We imagine that God should let us have our way. And when he doesn't, we resent him.

Feeling that way, we might cling to what is sometimes called the doctrine of "free will." This can be a misleading term, however, because our free will is limited in two significant ways.

① It's limited first because we're finite. Even when morally perfect, Adam and Eve weren't free to do whatever might come into their minds. Even if they wanted to, they couldn't fly, swim underwater for hours, or make themselves taller or shorter. There were a lot of things they weren't smart enough or strong enough to do. God alone is infinite, and therefore *God alone has a completely free will* that permits him to do whatever he wants (and which will always be in keeping with his flawless character).

② Second, our free will is further limited by our sin natures, although this limitation may be less obvious to us. *We're not just finite, we're fallen.*

Jesus said, "Everyone who sins is a slave to sin" (John 8:34), and slaves, by definition, have seriously restricted freedom. As sinners, we don't have the freedom to choose in exactly the same way Adam and Eve did. Our freedom still exists, but our fallenness greatly limits our capacity to obey God. Scripture tells us, and experience confirms, that sin holds us in bondage.

EXPANDING FREEDOM

It's true that those without Christ are tied to their sin; although they can modify many sinful behaviors, they can't escape the sin built into their nature. Without Christ, we remain spiritually separated from God and cannot earn our way to Heaven, but this doesn't mean we're as evil as we could possibly be, or that we lack any capacity to do anything good or worthwhile. Adulterers, thieves, the greedy, and gossipers can all risk their lives to save a child, which is surely a good thing.

But once we experience salvation in Christ, this not only changes our destiny in the afterlife, but also radically affects our capacity to do good and to resist evil in this life.

As believers, our justification by faith in Christ changes our legal status before God, satisfying the just demands of the law, by imputing our sins to Christ and Christ's righteousness to us (see Romans 3:21–26). In regeneration, God grants to the believer a new nature that, as he draws upon God's power, can overcome evil, giving him a greater freedom of choice than he had when he was in bondage to sin.

Regeneration renews the will, enabling us to make godly choices (see Philippians 2:13; 2 Thessalonians 3:5). God speaks of the "washing of regeneration and renewal of the Holy Spirit" (Titus 3:5, ESV). Once born again, believers cannot continue to sin as a lifestyle because of our new nature (see 1 John 3:9). Sin is still present in our lives (see Romans 6:11–14; 1 John 1:8–2:2). But we have supernatural power to overcome sin, for we've died to sin and are free from slavery to it (see Romans 6:6–9). God's Holy Spirit indwells us and helps us to obey him (see 2 Timothy 1:14).

Although there will always be certain limits on our human freedom of will, that freedom is expanded dramatically when we become united with Christ through faith in him. As Jesus expressed it, "If the Son sets you free, you will be free indeed" (John 8:36).

Meanwhile, in exercising our true freedom, we can also be assured that choosing what is good and right will always be to our advantage. Wrongdoing sometimes appears to offer benefits, and doing right may seem to bring serious disadvantages. But in the long run, often in this life and always in the afterlife, God rewards right choices and confers consequences for wrong ones.

"Do not be deceived: God cannot be mocked. A man reaps what he sows" (Galatians 6:7).

Justice may be delayed, but it always comes: "The sins of some men are obvious, reaching the place of judgment ahead of them; the sins of others trail behind them" (1 Timothy 5:24).

In a universe where God is Creator and Judge, doing good is always smart while doing evil is always stupid.

REAL CHOICES, REAL SOVEREIGNTY

Our thoughts about human free will should always be balanced with the reminder of God's sovereignty. Paul anticipates our natural response to his argument for God's sovereignty and election: "One of you will say to me: 'Then why does God still blame us? For who resists his will?' But who are you, O man, to talk back to God? 'Shall what is formed say to him who formed it, "Why did you make me like this?"' Does not the potter have the right to make out of the same lump of clay some pottery for noble purposes and some for common use?" (Romans 9:19–21). Scripture appeals here to *God's* free will, not mankind's; to Creator's rights, not creatures' rights.

But if everything on Earth takes place as God wills it, then why would he have agonized over the human evil that moved him to judge the Earth with the Flood? Why did Jesus weep over the death of Lazarus? Is it God's will, his actual *desire,* that sexual predators rape women and abuse children? No.

Since God can use evil for his glory, if I abstain from a sin or try to stop a sin, am I in danger of trying to thwart God's will? No, because God commands us to intervene to stop injustice, so that his moral will is done.

Scripture teaches that *humans make real choices* and that we must resist evil, yet *God remains sovereign* in a nonfatalistic way, offering us choices and encouraging us to pray to him to bring changes, and to do what we can to change our lives and the world itself. This may confuse us, but the Bible plainly teaches both truths.

We also see in Scripture that God wills things in two different senses. First, God has an ultimate decreed purpose. It was his will to create the world, it is his will to redeem his people, and it is his will to return and set up his eternal kingdom on a New Earth. No created being can thwart God's will: "Many are the plans in the mind of a man, but it is the purpose of the LORD that will stand" (Proverbs 19:21, ESV).

Second, God has a moral will reflected in his stated desires for us. For instance, "It is God's will that you should be sanctified: that you should avoid sexual immorality" (1 Thessalonians 4:3). Every immoral act is a violation of God's expressed desire.

God temporarily allows or permits things that are not in keeping with his will as reflected in his moral laws and character. We see this in Scriptures that use a variety of terms to describe God's relationship to evil, including *permit* and *allow.* For example, Old Testament laws speak of what to do when an ax head flies from its handle and kills someone. It allows for the ax wielder's life to be spared if he "does not do it intentionally, but God lets it happen" (Exodus 21:13). The choice of words indicates not that God *causes* the accident, but rather he "lets it happen." He causes much, but he remains totally sovereign even when he only allows rather than causes.

We find similar language in the New Testament—for example, in the incident where demons beg Jesus to send them into a herd of pigs, and we're told Jesus "gave them permission" (see Mark 5:12–13).

Sometimes God inhibits demonic and human choice by not permitting them to fulfill their evil desire. God tells Abimelech, "I have kept you from sinning against me" (Genesis 20:6). Jacob said of Laban, "God has not allowed him to harm me" (Genesis 31:7). When casting out demons, Jesus "would not allow them to speak" (Luke 4:41).

Dorothy Sayers wrote,

> "Why doesn't God smite this dictator dead?" is a question a little remote from us. Why, madam, did he not strike you dumb and imbecile before you uttered that baseless and unkind slander the day before yesterday? Or me, before I behaved with such a cruel lack of consideration to that well-meaning friend? And why sir, did he not cause your hand to rot off at the wrist before you signed your name to that dirty bit of financial trickery? You did not quite mean that? But why not? Your misdeeds and mine are none the less repellent because our opportunities for doing damage are less spectacular than those of some other people. Do you suggest that your doings and mine are too trivial for God to bother about? That cuts both ways; for in that case, it would make precious little difference to his creation if he wiped us both out tomorrow.[3]

We may sometimes be disturbed by this truth that God sometimes allows or permits bad things to happen, but properly understood it should be comforting. What should be disturbing is the popular, but false, notion that God stands passively by while Satan, evildoers, diseases, and random accidents ruin the lives of his beloved children.

Divine Purpose

The mistaken idea that events happen randomly outside God's control sets us up for a lifetime of "what ifs" and "if onlys."

None of our actions lies outside the reach of God's governance. For this we should feel deeply grateful. Otherwise we could wonder, *What if the doctor had run the right tests or looked at the x-rays more carefully two years ago?* Or, *What if I'd stopped to make the phone call? If the line had been shorter at the grocery store? If I hadn't had that five-minute conversation before leaving? Then I wouldn't have been at that intersection when the drunk driver ran the light and smashed my car, and then my wife wouldn't have died.*

If the world is as random as some theologians suggest, it would seem that people, demons, and luck determine our destinies. We can drive ourselves crazy with such thoughts. Or, instead, we can follow the lead of Scripture and embrace the belief that a sovereign God is accomplishing eternal purposes in the midst of painful and even tragic events. If we trust God, we affirm his greatness, his love for us, and our love for him, bringing him glory.

God calls us neither to victimization nor fatalism, but to faith in his character and promises.

Notes

1. Nancy Guthrie, *Holding On to Hope* (Carol Stream, IL: Tyndale, 2002), 39.
2. Margaret Clarkson, *Grace Grows Best in Winter* (Grand Rapids, MI: Eerdmans, 1984), 40–41.
3. Dorothy L. Sayers, "The Triumph of Easter," in *Creed or Chaos* (London: Methuen, 1954).

8

Are We Promised Prosperity?

*Recovering a Biblical View
of Health and Wealth*

A woman lay dying of cancer. She had based her life on the
"health and wealth" teaching that says God will bless with
material abundance and good health those who obey him and lay
claim to his promises. But now she looked into a camera during an
interview and said, "I've lost my faith." She felt bitter that God had
"broken his promises."

This woman correctly realized that the god she'd followed does
not exist. But the God of the Bible had *not* let her down; her church
and its preachers had done that. The simple truth is that God never
made the promises she thought he'd broken.

SURPRISING PROMISES

Here's the sad truth: *prosperity theology has poisoned the church and
undermined our ability to deal with evil and suffering.*

Some churches today have no place for pain. Those people

who say God has healed them get the microphone, while those who continue to suffer are shamed into silence or ushered out the back door.

The Bible makes promises we don't want God to keep. For instance, "It has been granted to you on behalf of Christ not only to believe on him, but also to suffer for him" (Philippians 1:29).

"In the world you will have tribulation," Jesus pledged (John 16:33, ESV). "Everyone who wants to live a godly life in Christ Jesus will suffer persecution" (2 Timothy 3:12, NLT). They may not be our favorite memory verses, but we should trust these promises as surely as we trust John 3:16.

The first story of the post-Fall world is Cain's murder of Abel, a righteous man who pleased God and suffered as a direct result. Noah, Abraham, Joseph, Moses, David, Daniel, Shadrach, Meshach, Abednego, and nearly all the prophets weren't just righteous people who happened to suffer. Rather, they suffered *because* they were righteous.

This continues in the New Testament, with Jesus as the prime example. Jesus said John the Baptist was the greatest of men (see Luke 7:28). Soon thereafter evildoers imprisoned then murdered John and mockingly displayed his head on a platter (see Matthew 14:6–12). What could be more utterly contradictory to the health and wealth gospel?

The Holy Spirit had hardly descended before wicked men stoned Stephen to death. Herod Agrippa beheaded James; later, Nero beheaded Paul. Tradition says Peter and Andrew were crucified; Matthew died a martyr; a lance killed Thomas; and Pharisees threw James the son of Alpheus from the temple, then stoned him and dashed his brains out with a club. First Peter is an entire book devoted to Christians suffering injustices for the sake of Christ.

Even at its best, the ancient world offered a hard life. Christians *routinely* suffered.

They still do. Even Christians who don't suffer persecution still pull weeds, experience pain in childbirth, become ill, and die, just like everyone else.

Prosperity theology's claims are so obviously opposed to countless biblical passages that it is difficult to imagine, apart from the deceptive powers of Satan, how so many Christians could actually believe them.

The truth is that if you are a Christian, God will deliver you from *eternal* suffering. And he will deliver you *through* your present suffering, though not always *from* it.

We should see our suffering as God keeping his promises, not violating them:

> Dear friends, do not be surprised at the painful trial you are
> suffering, as though something strange were happening to
> you. But *rejoice* that you participate in the sufferings of
> Christ, so that you may be overjoyed when his glory is
> revealed. (1 Peter 4:12–13)

Suffering—whether from persecution, accidents, or illnesses—shouldn't surprise us. God has promised it. And when it comes, people should lose their faith in false doctrine, not in God.

DIVINE DISEASE

Of course we should seek to be healthy, both physically and mentally. But we miss out on a great deal if we fail to see that God can also accomplish his purposes when we lose our health and he chooses not to heal us.

Julia was a powerful woman who flaunted her beauty and wealth. Her volatile temper and sharp tongue put people in their place and left a trail of damaged relationships.

Then, in her midforties, Julia was diagnosed with an aggressive cancer. Despite treatment, the disease progressed. Doctors said she had less than a year to live.

As time passed, Julia underwent a remarkable change. Her diagnosis frightened her; she sought spiritual counsel, started reading the New Testament, confessed her sins, and gave her life to Jesus Christ. She wrote letters, made phone calls, invited people for coffee, and sought forgiveness from the many she'd hurt. She did all she could to restore relationships with family and others. She made peace with her ex-husband, grew close to her children, and developed a loving circle of Christian friends.

Several weeks before she died, Julia told her pastor that she considered her cancer to be a love gift from God. She believed the Lord had used her disease to draw her to himself. Julia said she would gladly exchange all her years of beauty, wealth, and influence for the two years of illness that taught her the unspeakable joy of loving Jesus and loving others.[1]

In contrast to Julia, however, many people with a terminal diagnosis spend the remainder of their lives searching for a scientific cure or a spiritual healing or both. I don't, of course, fault sick people for seeking a cure! But, like Julia, we should focus our energies not simply on *avoiding* death, but on investing our time in *preparing* for it—getting right with God and ministering to others. While resisting death and fighting for life can be virtuous, it can also degenerate into idolatry if staying alive here becomes more important than anything else.

Apostolic Illness

If God heals you, rejoice! God can and does heal, and we should celebrate his mercy. But if you've prayed for healing and not received it, take heart—you're in good company!

In the early church, committed Christian leaders routinely endured diseases and other suffering. Paul once had to leave his friend Trophimus behind because of sickness (see 2 Timothy 4:20). Another beloved friend, Epaphroditus, became gravely ill (see Philippians 2:25–30). Paul's spiritual son Timothy had frequent stomach disorders, for which Paul told him to drink a little wine for medicinal purposes (see 1 Timothy 5:23).

Those who claim anyone with enough faith can be healed must believe they have greater faith than Paul and his fellow missionaries. Second Corinthians 12:7 gives us a striking picture. We see God sending a physical disability for his purposes and Satan sending the same disability for his. Paul says, "To keep me from being conceited because of these surpassingly great revelations [of heaven], there was given me a thorn in my flesh." If the text stopped here, it would be obvious who gave the thorn in the flesh—God, who wanted to keep Paul from becoming conceited.

But Paul continues to describe the thorn in the flesh as "a messenger of Satan, to torment me." Two supernatural beings, adamantly opposed to each other, are said in a single verse to have distinct purposes in sending Paul a thorn in the flesh. God's purpose is not to torment him, but to keep him from becoming conceited; Satan's purpose is to torment him, in the hope of turning him from God. Whose purpose will be accomplished? Who will win?

Remember, God and the devil aren't equal opposites! God is the infinite and holy Creator; Satan is the finite and fallen creature. Satan and God intend the same suffering for entirely different purposes, but in the end God's purpose triumphs in Paul's life.

Paul says in this passage that he asked God three times to remove the thorn—the disease or disability—but God refused. He did, however, reveal a purpose behind Paul's unanswered prayer: "My grace is sufficient for you, for my power is made perfect in weakness" (2 Corinthians 12:9).

How did Paul respond? He said he rejoiced in his afflictions (see verses 9–10). Why? Because he knew God had a sovereign and loving purpose.

Joseph's brothers intended his suffering for evil; God intended it for good (see Genesis 50:20). Satan intended Job's suffering for evil; God intended it for good. Satan intended Jesus' suffering for evil; God intended it for good. Satan intended Paul's suffering for evil; God intended it for good. In each case, God's purpose prevailed.

Satan intends your suffering for evil; God intends it for good.

Whose purpose in your suffering will prevail? Whose purpose are you furthering?

Satan attempts to destroy your faith, while God invites you to draw near to him and rely upon his sovereign grace to sustain you.

If we recognize God's sovereignty even over Satan's work, it radically alters our perspective. Some Christians constantly assign this mishap to Satan, that one to evil people, another to themselves, still others to God. Sometimes they are right, but how can they be sure which is which? Second Corinthians 12 makes clear that God works through *everything* that comes our way, no matter whom it comes from. If God can use for good "a messenger of Satan," then surely he can use for good a car accident or your employer's unreasonable expectations.

You might not know whether demons, or human genetics under the Fall, or a doctor's poor decision, or God's direct hand have brought about your disease, but you know as much as you need to—that God is sovereign. Whether he heals your body now or waits until the resurrection to heal you, he desires to achieve his own good purpose in you.

By undermining these great truths, the health and wealth gospel distorts the true gospel of God's sovereign grace.

DEATH'S INEVITABILITY

Let me share some bad news: I have a fatal disease. I'm terminal. I'm going to die. But the news is even worse. *You* have the same fatal disease—mortality. You're going to die too.

Nothing could be more obvious. Yet somehow we don't take it to heart, do we?

Have you noticed that there are no 120-year-old faith healers? What does that tell you?

Emmanuel Ndikumana explained why he returned home to Burundi when the Hutu-Tutsi conflict threatened his life. In revenge for atrocities, Tutsis already had killed his Hutu father and grandfather. Emmanuel told me, "I do not condemn those who fled; I understand. But I felt I should not treasure safety. The only way for me to prove to my people that I believed the gospel was to return and suffer with them. If I fear death as unbelievers do, I have nothing to offer unbelievers. Only when you are free from the fear of death are you really free."

The apostle Paul in the Bible had it right: "Christ will be exalted in my body, whether by life or by death. For to me, to live is Christ and to die is gain" (Philippians 1:20–21).

WEALTH'S PURPOSE

When it comes to wealth, a further fault of prosperity theology is that it encourages us to spend on ourselves the unprecedented wealth God has entrusted to us for relieving world suffering. A reporter asked Mother Teresa, "When a baby dies alone in a Calcutta alley, where is God?" Her response? "God is there, suffering with that baby. The question really is where are *you*?"[2]

As God laments over the suffering child, so should we. God's heart is stirred to bring help to the needy—normally by providing his people with the means to help. When we stand in his presence, Christ can show us the scars on his hands and feet and say, "Here's what *I* did about evil and suffering." What will we say when he asks, "What did *you* do?"

Some Christian leaders think living affluently gives them credibility, but the Bible equates good leadership with perseverance in suffering. Paul argued for his own credibility as God's servant based on his "troubles, hardships and distresses; in beatings, imprisonments and riots; in hard work, sleepless nights and hunger" (2 Corinthians 6:4–5).

Neither Christian leaders nor lay believers should expect God to continue making us affluent. If we don't follow God when he prospers us, he may take away our national and personal prosperity to bring us to repentance and dependence (see Deuteronomy 28:47–48). When will we learn that God doesn't give us greater wealth to increase our standard of living, but to increase our standard of giving?

HIGHER PURPOSE

Disease, hardship, poverty, suffering, and death are part of the Curse; one day Jesus will reverse that Curse...but not yet.

And while God assures us that he'll one day remove all suffering and sorrow, he'll do so as a by-product of his highest purpose for us: "The LORD will be your everlasting light, and your God will be your glory" (Isaiah 60:19). If we come to see the purpose of the universe as God's long-term glory rather than our short-term happiness, then we'll undergo a critical paradigm shift in tackling the problem of evil and suffering.

The world has gone terribly wrong.

God is going to fix it.

For his eternal glory.

And for our eternal good.

Notes

1. Adapted from Alice Gray, *Treasures for Women Who Hope* (Nashville: W Publishing, 2005), 51–52.
2. John G. Stackhouse Jr., *Can God Be Trusted?* (Oxford: Oxford University Press, 1998), 67.

9

The World We Long For

*Exploring God's Eternal Solution
to Evil and Suffering*

As a teenager held in a World War II Japanese prison camp in China, Margaret Holder felt the almost unbearable pain of forced separation from her family. But as the war progressed, American planes dropped barrels of food and supplies. When Nanci and I spoke with her forty-five years later, Margaret recalled with delight "care packages falling from the sky."

One day an American plane flew low and dropped more of those wonderful food barrels. But as the barrels neared the ground, the captives realized something had changed. Her eyes bright, Margaret told us, "This time the barrels had legs!" The sky rained American soldiers, parachuting down to rescue them. Margaret and several hundred children rushed out of the camp past the Japanese guards, who offered no resistance. Free for the first time in six years, they ran to the soldiers, throwing themselves on their rescuers, hugging and kissing them.

Yes, I know those six years of confinement and separation from family caused great suffering for that young girl and her family. But I also know what I saw in the eyes and heard in the voice of Margaret Holder almost half a century later. She exuded sheer *joy,* a joy

she simply never would have known without the suffering that pre-
ceded it.

In the sixty-five years since their dramatic rescue from that
prison camp, most of those children have died. Those who loved
Jesus are now with him. Imagine their joy in being reunited *yet again*
with their parents and with some of their rescuers! But this time the
reunion will never end. And this time they will live forever with Jesus,
the source of all joy.

If the soldiers rejoiced in rescuing those children, think how
God rejoices in rescuing us. Whether he returns in the sky to liberate us or draws us to himself through our deaths, he will indeed rescue us and unite us with him and our loved ones. He'll liberate us
from a world under the Curse and take us home—where evil and
suffering can never touch us, his beloved children, again.

A Two-Part Solution

When the New Testament discusses suffering, it repeatedly puts
Heaven before the eyes of believers. The assurance of Heaven's compensation for our present life should give us an eternal perspective.

Of course the New Testament also speaks at length about Hell.
Heaven and Hell represent God's eternal two-part solution to the
problem of the righteous presently suffering and the wicked presently
prospering.

Hell as Justice

Sometimes we cry out for true and lasting justice, then fault God for
taking evil too seriously by administering eternal punishment. But we
can't have it both ways. To argue against Hell is to argue against justice.

(LOOK AHEAD)

When most people speak of what a terrible notion Hell is, they talk as if it involves the suffering of innocent people. That would indeed be terribly unjust—but nowhere does the Bible suggest the innocent will spend a single moment in Hell.

Without Hell, justice would never overtake the unrepentant tyrants in world history who are responsible for murdering millions. Perpetrators of evil throughout the ages would get away with murder—and rape, and torture, and every evil. If there's no Hell, there's no justice.

Even if we may acknowledge Hell as a necessary and just punishment for evildoers, however, we rarely see *ourselves* as worthy of Hell. After all, *we* are not ruthless dictators or serial killers or raging terrorists.

We are utterly unqualified to assess how often we sin and how bad our sins are. Sin means nothing to those who are riddled with it. If you have had leprosy all your life and have never been treated for it, leprosy doesn't seem remarkable to you. You've never known anything else. We've never known anything but being sinful. To step outside ourselves and see our sin for what it is, is impossible. If not for the testimony of God's Word, as well as the conscience God has put in his image-bearers, we might have no clue of our sinfulness.

"There is no one righteous, not even one" (Romans 3:10). We consider ourselves "good people," but we're wrong. We each have our preferred ways of sinning, whether as prostitutes, porn addicts, materialists, gossips, or the self-righteous. But we all are sinners who deserve Hell. Guilty people can always rationalize sin, but Hell exists because *sin has no excuse.*

Hell is morally good, because a good God must punish evil.

That sounds like nonsense to Hell-hating moderns, but it makes perfect sense if only we would recognize and hate *evil* for what it is, an egregious offense against an absolutely righteous Creator. If eternal Hell seems to us disproportionate punishment, it is precisely because we have no sense of proportion about what it means to sin against an infinitely holy being.

Contrary to many people's logic, God's justice doesn't demand that he give people a second chance after death, because God gives us thousands of chances before death. The chance to respond to the message of creation that cries out, "There is a God!" is repeated multiple times daily, over a lifetime. Every breath is an opportunity to respond to a conscience that convicts people of their guilt.

If we better understood both God's nature and our own, we would not feel shocked that some people go to Hell. (Where else could sinners go?) Rather, we would feel shocked—as perhaps the angels do—that any fallen human would be permitted into Heaven. Unholy as we are in ourselves, we're disqualified to claim that infinite holiness cannot demand everlasting punishment.

JESUS AND HELL

In the Bible, Jesus spoke more about Hell than anyone else did. And he couldn't have painted a bleaker picture.

Jesus referred to Hell as a real place and described it in graphic terms (see Matthew 10:28; 13:40–42; Mark 9:43–48). He spoke of a fire that burns but doesn't consume, an undying worm that eats away at the damned, and a lonely and foreboding darkness. Christ says the unsaved "will be thrown outside, into the darkness, where there will be weeping and gnashing of teeth" (Matthew 8:12). Jesus taught that an unbridgeable chasm separates the wicked in Hell from the righteous in paradise. The wicked suffer terribly, remain conscious, retain their desires and memories, long for relief, cannot find comfort, cannot leave their torment, and have no hope (see Luke 16:19–31).

Jesus' words tell us plainly that Hell is a place of eternal punishment—*not* annihilation. However, some Christians believe that upon dying, or at the final judgment, those without Christ will simply cease to exist. Such annihilation is an attractive teaching compared to the alternative—I would gladly embrace it, were it taught in Scripture. But though I've tried, I just can't find it there.

On the contrary, Jesus said, "Then they will go away to eternal punishment, but the righteous to eternal life" (Matthew 25:46). Here in the same sentence, Christ uses the word "eternal" *(aionos)* to describe the duration of *both* Heaven and Hell. Thus, according to our Lord, if some will consciously experience Heaven forever, then some must consciously experience Hell forever.

We may pride ourselves in thinking we're too loving to believe in Hell. But in saying this, we blaspheme, for we claim to be more loving than Jesus—more loving than the One who with outrageous love took upon himself the full penalty for our sin.

C. S. Lewis said of Hell, "There is no doctrine which I would more willingly remove from Christianity than this, if it lay in my power. But it has the full support of Scripture and, specially, of Our Lord's own words; it has always been held by Christendom; and it has the support of reason."[1]

Even among those who believe in Hell, the vast majority do not believe they're going there. Our culture considers Heaven the default destination. (When did you last attend a funeral in which a speaker pictured the departed in Hell?)

But since "all have sinned and fall short of the glory of God" (Romans 3:23) and "without holiness no one will see the Lord" (Hebrews 12:14), none of us will enter the presence of an infinitely holy God unless something in us radically changes. <u>Until our sin problem gets resolved, Hell will remain our default destination.</u> And that sin problem can be resolved only through faith in Christ. Only then will we find the doorway opened into Heaven.

CERTAIN RESURRECTION

Those who believe in Christ could more accurately call our present existence the *beforelife* rather than calling Heaven the *afterlife*. Life doesn't merely continue in Heaven; it emerges at last to its intended fullness.

Dinesh D'Souza writes,

> The only way for us to really triumph over evil and suffering is to live forever in a place where those things do not exist. It is the claim of Christianity that there is such a place and that it is available to all who seek it. No one can deny that, if this claim is true, then evil and suffering are exposed as temporary hardships and injustices. They are as transient as our brief, mortal lives. In that case God has shown us a way to prevail over evil and suffering, which are finally overcome in the life to come.[2]

Only the resurrection can solve the gigantic problems of this world—and resurrection cannot come without death.

Many Bible-believing Christians today are crippled by their unbiblical view of the life to come. This is why I have written at length on the subject of Heaven.[3] Ironically, there are Christians who would die rather than deny the resurrection, yet they actually don't understand or believe what the doctrine of the resurrection means.

The resurrection God promises in the Bible means there is continuity from this life to the next. It means we can say what Job did: "After my skin has been destroyed, yet in my flesh I will see God; I myself will see him with my own eyes—I, and not another" (19:26–27).

If we don't grasp the principle of redemptive continuity, we cannot understand the nature of resurrection. Anthony Hoekema writes, "There must be continuity, for otherwise there would be little point in speaking about a resurrection at all. The calling into existence of a completely new set of people totally different from the present inhabitants of the earth would not be a resurrection."[4]

The doctrine of the resurrection guarantees that not only our bodies but the Earth itself, the very best parts about this world, will carry over to the next, with none of the bad. Hence, what we forgo here will prove no great loss, and every aspect of being with Christ in the world to come will be great gain. As missionary martyr Jim Elliot put it, "He is no fool who gives what he cannot keep to gain what he cannot lose."

Without Christ's resurrection and what it means—an eternal future for fully restored human beings, dwelling with Christ on a fully restored Earth—all the promises of Christianity vanish like smoke in a stiff wind. As Paul says, "If Christ has not been raised, your faith is futile; you are still in your sins.... We are to be pitied more than all men" (1 Corinthians 15:17, 19). Thankfully, our resurrection is certain because of Christ's resurrection, and the promises of an all-knowing and all-powerful God.

No Suffering, No Glory

In order to share Christ's honor forever on the New Earth, we must share his heartaches temporarily on the fallen Earth.

Paul states it this way: "Now if we are children, then we are heirs—heirs of God and co-heirs with Christ, if indeed we share in his sufferings in order that we may also share in his glory" (Romans 8:17). We'll become Christ's heirs and share in his glory *if* we participate in his sufferings.

F. F. Bruce writes, "It is not merely that the glory is a compensation for the suffering; it actually grows out of the suffering. There is an organic relation between the two for the believer as surely as there was for his Lord."[5]

When Christ sets up his eternal kingdom, he'll banish evil and suffering. We'll remember both, just as the martyrs in heaven spoken of in Revelation 6:9–11 remember. But our memories won't hurt us; they will instead prompt our gratitude and worship and anticipation of all the goodness that still awaits us.

Our happiness in Heaven won't be dependent on our ignorance of what happened on Earth—it will be enhanced by our changed *perspective* on it.

NO SIN, NO SUFFERING

On a planet without sin, there can be no suffering.

The new nature that will be fully ours in Heaven—the very righteousness of Christ—will never sin. That we won't ever sin in Heaven does *not* mean we won't have free will. Remember, though "God cannot be tempted by evil" (James 1:13), no being has greater free choice than he does. It is not in his nature to sin, and it will not be in our natures to sin.

Once we become what the sovereign God has made us to be in Christ, and once we see him as he is, then we'll see all things—including sin and suffering—for what they are. God won't need to restrain us from evil. It will have absolutely no appeal. It will be, literally, unthinkable. The memory of evil and suffering in this life will serve as an eternal reminder of sin's horrors and emptiness. Having known sin and having become fully righteous, we will no longer want to sin. "Sin? Been there, done that. Seen how ugly and disastrous it was."

God's people "are looking forward to a new heaven and a new earth, the home of righteousness" (2 Peter 3:13).

In that redeemed universe, God's righteousness will be our lifeblood, Jesus will be our passion, and joy will be the air we breathe.

Notes

1. C. S. Lewis, *The Problem of Pain* (New York: Macmillan, 1962), 118.
2. Dinesh D'Souza, *What's So Great About Christianity* (Washington DC: Regnery, 2007), 291.
3. See Randy Alcorn, *Heaven* (Carol Stream, IL: Tyndale, 2004).
4. Anthony A. Hoekema, *The Bible and the Future* (Grand Rapids, MI: Eerdmans, 1979), 251.
5. F. F. Bruce, *The Epistle of Paul to the Romans* (Downers Grove, IL: InterVarsity, 1985), 168.

10

Wanting More Clarity

Wrestling with the Reasons for Our Suffering

When I was seventeen years old and had known Christ for less than two years, I experienced what I believe was a miracle. Driving at fifty miles an hour, I was about to crash. All I could see in front of me, top to bottom and side to side, was the yellow of a school bus, which pulled in front of me from a side road, but which I didn't see until a split second before impact.

But the impact never happened. My tiny Hillman Minx car should have smashed into that bus. I still can't explain why it didn't, and why instead my car ended up slowing to a stop in a cauliflower field, undamaged.

I was deeply grateful, of course, and am to this day. God was faithful, God was gracious, God saved my life. All that is true.

But I soon discovered things don't always turn out that way for God's children.

A few months later my good friend Greg Coffey, who had come to faith in Christ just a year before, had a terrible accident. Smart and athletic and with a promising future, Greg was swinging on a big tree branch, over a fence. The branch broke, and he was impaled upon a metal fence post. I sat on the floor outside intensive care, begging God to save Greg's life.

When a nurse let me into his room, I saw my friend fighting for his life. I was convinced it could not be God's will for him to die. He was growing closer to God every day, studying God's Word, sharing his faith. Greg had a bright future in God's service. I *knew* God would heal him. I couldn't have been more certain; I've never had greater faith.

Two days later Greg died.

I was stunned, in disbelief. How could this happen?

Couldn't the same God who kept me from smashing into that school bus have kept that tree limb from breaking, kept Greg from falling on that metal post? If God appointed angels to preserve my life, why didn't he appoint angels to preserve Greg's life?

Sometimes we make the foolish assumption that our heavenly Father has no right to insist that we trust him unless he makes his infinite wisdom completely understandable to us. What we call the problem of evil is often the problem of our finite and fallen understanding. It was the hardest lesson I'd ever had to learn.

APPARENT IMPOSSIBILITIES

Gregory Boyd writes, "It's very difficult to see how some of the more horrendous episodes of evil in this world contribute to a higher good."[1] His conclusion is, therefore, that they don't.

I agree "it's very difficult to see." It may well be *impossible* to see. But the question isn't whether we can see it but whether God can do things we cannot see.

Not only Scripture but human experience sometimes testifies to the surprising good God can bring out of evil and suffering. God calls upon us to trust that he'll work all evil and suffering in our lives for good. We can learn to trust God in the worst of circumstances, even for what we cannot currently see—indeed, that's the very nature of biblical faith (see Hebrews 11:8, 13, 27, 32–39).

We're not positioned to know how much suffering is required to accomplish the best eternal purposes, nor how much it might hinder those purposes for God to make himself obvious.

Is it possible that all past, present, and future suffering is somehow necessary for God to accomplish the greater good his people will enjoy for all eternity? If you think this cannot be the case, why? If you're certain it can't be, have you never been wrong?

Philosopher Thomas Morris writes,

> Many times…people don't have a clue as to what exactly they would do about the most pressing problems of their own city if they were mayor, or concerning the greatest difficulty facing their state if they were governor. They would probably be quite hesitant if asked how, precisely, they would solve the greatest national crises if they were president, but they have no hesitation whatsoever in venturing to declare how they would solve what may be the single most troubling cosmic religious problem if they were God.[2]

We who have not formed galaxies and quasars and fashioned worlds shouldn't be so quick to tell God how to run his universe.

CHILDISH CURIOSITY

Usually children don't fully comprehend why we discipline them, make them clean their rooms, take them to the dentist, or refuse to allow them to eat all the candy they want. One day, when they grow up, they'll get it.

And so will we.   DO WE HAVE TO GET IT

John Stott tells a story about billions of people seated on a great plain before God's throne. Most shrank back, while some crowded to the front, raising angry voices.

"Can God judge us? How can he know about suffering?" snapped one woman, ripping a sleeve to reveal a tattooed number from a Nazi concentration camp. "We endured terror… beatings… torture… death!"

Other sufferers expressed their complaints against God for the evil and suffering he had permitted. What did God know of weeping, hunger, and hatred? God leads a sheltered life in Heaven, they said.

Someone from Hiroshima, people born deformed, others murdered, each sent forward a leader. They concluded that before God could judge them, he should be sentenced to live on Earth as a man to endure the suffering they had endured. Then they pronounced a sentence:

Let him be born a Jew. Let the legitimacy of his birth be doubted. Let his close friends betray him. Let him face false charges. Let a prejudiced jury try him and a cowardly judge convict him. Let him be tortured. Let him be utterly alone. Then, bloody and forsaken, let him die.

The room grew silent after the sentence against God had been pronounced. No one moved, and a weight fell on each face.

For suddenly, all knew that God already had served his sentence.[3]

Some people can't believe God would create a world in which people would suffer so much. <u>Isn't it more remarkable that God would create a world in which no one would suffer more than he</u>?

That God did this willingly, with ancient premeditation, is all the more remarkable. Jesus said, "<u>I lay down my life for the sheep.</u>... <u>No one takes it from me, but I lay it down of my own accord</u>" (John 10:15, 18). When the son of a friend of mine died, I asked him about life in the aftermath of this tragedy. He wrote these words to me: "I think it's good for books to offer biblical guidance on suffering and evil, but the greatest comfort for me has been to focus on God. I'm not as concerned about the whys. When you know him, it's okay. I can trust him with what I don't know. <u>That's what brings me back to the Bible.</u>"

<u>(In our times of suffering, God doesn't give answers as much as he gives himself.)</u> And already, in the Bible, he has revealed more than enough of himself to give us solid reasons for faith—yet not enough to make our faith unnecessary.

An Unlikely Recipe

THE RESULT ISN'T ALWAYS WHAT WE EXPECT

One of the most arresting statements in Scripture is this one: "And we know that for those who love God <u>*all things*</u> work together for good, for those who are called according to his purpose" (Romans 8:28, ESV). Different translations of this passage suggest different nuances: for those who love God, "all things work together for good" (ESV, KJV); "in all things God works for the good" (NIV); "God causes all things to work together for good" (NASB). In each case there's an omni-inclusiveness in "all things."

The context of this passage shows that in the midst of a world that groans under suffering and evil, God's main concern is conforming his children to the image of Christ. And he works through the challenging circumstances of our lives to help develop that Christlikeness in us. We can be assured that whatever difficulty he has allowed in our lives has been Father-filtered, through his fingers of wisdom and love.

The apostle Paul wrote Romans 8:28, and his life was filled with hardship, beatings, shipwrecks, cold, hunger, and sorrow. Paul was neither naive about suffering nor isolated from it.

Perhaps the greatest test of whether we who are Christ's followers believe the truth of this verse is to identify the very worst things that have ever happened to us, then to ask whether we believe God will in the end somehow use those things for our good. The Bible is emphatic that *he will.* We have no reason to think he'll be any less trustworthy concerning this than with any other promise he has made.

Notice that the verse doesn't say that each thing we experience *is* good in itself, or works for good on its own, but rather that God causes them all to work *together* for our good, under his sovereign hand. In other words, Romans 8:28 declares a cumulative and ultimate good, not an individual or immediate good.

Before my mother made a cake, she used to set each of the ingredients on the kitchen counter. One day, I decided to experiment. I tasted all the individual ingredients for a chocolate cake. Baking powder. Baking soda. Raw eggs. Vanilla extract. I discovered that *almost everything that goes into a cake tastes terrible by itself.* But a remarkable metamorphosis took place when my mother mixed those ingredients in the right amounts and baked them together. The cake tasted delicious.

In a similar way, each trial and apparent tragedy tastes bitter to us. Romans 8:28 doesn't tell me "it is good" if my leg breaks, or my house burns down, or I am robbed and beaten, or my child dies. Rather, God carefully measures out and mixes all the ingredients together, including the most bitter ones, and in the end, as measured after life here is done, produces a wonderful final product.

Paul goes on in Romans 8 to explain the basis on which he can claim that God works everything together for our good: "For those God foreknew he also predestined to be conformed to the likeness of his Son" (verse 29). Although we may define our good in terms of what brings us health and happiness now, God defines it in terms of what makes us more like Jesus. If God answered all our prayers to be delivered from evil and suffering, then he would be delivering us from Christlikeness.

Despite all appearances, God can redeem the most terrible situations. If Romans 8:28 means anything, surely it means that.

INCREASED GODLINESS

Mountain climbers could save time and energy if they reached the summit in a helicopter, but their ultimate purpose is conquest, not efficiency. Sure, they want to reach a goal, but they desire to do so the hard way, by testing and deepening their character, discipline, and resolve.

God could create scientists, mathematicians, athletes, and musicians. He doesn't. He creates children who take on those roles over a long process. God doesn't make us fully Christlike the moment we're born again. He conforms us to the image of Christ gradually, over a period of time: "And we, who with unveiled faces all reflect the Lord's glory, are being transformed into his likeness with ever-increasing glory" (2 Corinthians 3:18).

In our spiritual lives, as in our professional lives, and in sports and hobbies, we improve and excel by handling failure and learning from it. Only in cultivating discipline, endurance, and patience do we find satisfaction and reward. And those qualities are most developed through some form of suffering.

For turning us toward God, sometimes nothing works like suffering. C. S. Lewis said, "God whispers to us in our pleasures, speaks in our conscience, but shouts in our pains: it is His megaphone to rouse a deaf world."[4]

Richard Baxter wrote, "Suffering so unbolts the door of the heart, that the Word hath easier entrance."[5] God uses suffering to bring us to the end of ourselves and back to Christ. And that's worth any cost.

Jesus said, "It is not the healthy who need a doctor, but the sick. I have not come to call the righteous, but sinners to repentance" (Luke 5:31–32). We need a cure, one that may require nasty-tasting medicine, painful surgery, and rigorous physical therapy. But without the pain, we won't even realize we're sick.

The pornography addict will tell himself nothing's wrong until he ends up losing his job, his wife, and his children. He cannot gain freedom until he faces the horrific consequences of his sin. To hate suffering is easy; to hate sin is not.

Instead of blaming doctors, drunk drivers, and criminals for our suffering, we should look for what God can accomplish through it—and trust him for the good he can bring from all suffering.

C. S. Lewis spoke of God's discipline this way:

But suppose that what you are up against is a surgeon whose intentions are wholly good. The kinder and more conscientious he is, the more inexorably he will go on cutting. If he yielded to your entreaties, if he stopped before the operation was complete, all the pain up to that point would have been useless…. What do people mean when they say, "I am not afraid of God because I know He is good"? Have they never even been to a dentist?[6]

I should clarify that God never punishes us to make us atone for our sins. He doesn't call on us to repeat Christ's atonement, but accept it. "The punishment that brought us peace was upon him" (Isaiah 53:5). But for us to be transformed increasingly into Christ's likeness, we *need* God's correction: "He disciplines us for our good, that we may share his holiness. For the moment all discipline seems painful rather than pleasant, but later it yields the peaceful fruit of righteousness to those who have been trained by it" (Hebrews 12:10–11, ESV).

INCREASED FAITH

Suffering exposes idols in our lives. It uncovers our trust in God-substitutes and declares our need to transfer our trust to the only One who can bear its weight. God laments, "My people have committed two sins: They have forsaken me, the spring of living water, and have dug their own cisterns, broken cisterns that cannot hold water" (Jeremiah 2:13).

We may imagine God as our genie who comes to do our bidding. Suffering wakes us up to the fact that we serve him, not he us. Diseases, accidents, and natural disasters remind us of our extreme vulnerability; life is out of our control.

We must relinquish our belief that we can prevent all bad things from happening. God reminds us, "The earth is the LORD's, and everything in it, the world, and all who live in it" (Psalm 24:1). What we think belongs to us really doesn't: "'The silver is mine and the gold is mine,' declares the LORD Almighty" (Haggai 2:8). We don't even belong to ourselves: "You are not your own; you were bought at a price" (1 Corinthians 6:19–20).

We should repeatedly tell our Lord, "This house is yours. The money, this body, and these children belong to you. You own the title deed; you own the rights; you have the power of life and death."

It becomes much easier to trust God when we understand that what he takes away belonged to him in the first place (see Job 1:21).

A victim of a great evil told me, "I discovered in myself the spirit of entitlement. I learned that God wasn't going to go down my checklist of happiness and fulfill it. I learned what it meant to surrender to his will. Before, I wanted certain gifts from him; now I want him." Near the end of our conversation she said something just as powerful: "I have thought, if this was going to happen to someone, it was better for it to happen to me, with my faith in God, than to happen to a twelve-year-old or an elderly person, or to anyone without Christ." She continued, "I've come through this with an absolute confidence in God. I know he'll walk with me through the rest of my life. I've been through the valley of the shadow of death, and he was with me. Because he's been faithful in all I've gone through, I have less to be afraid of now."

INCREASED GRATITUDE

It seems counterintuitive to give thanks in suffering, but God commands it, and countless people have benefited from it.

Elisabeth Elliot, one of my heroes, writes, "On one of those terrible days during my husband's cancer, when he could hardly bear the pain or the thought of yet another treatment, and I could hardly bear to bear it with him, we remarked on how wonderful it would be to have just a single ordinary day."[7]

How many of us fail to express gratitude for those ordinary days, wishing instead for something better? If you've had a single ordinary day recently, why not thank God for it? Don't wait for an extraordinary day when you feel wonderful and everything goes your way. That day may not come. Yet if it does, God's hand is in it just as it is in all other days, both good and bad.

Cultivating thankfulness today will allow us to cling to God's goodness and mercy in our darkest hours. Those hours lie ahead of us—but beyond them stretch unending millennia of inexpressible joy that we'll appreciate more deeply because of these fleeting days of darkness.

HOPE

INCREASED HUMILITY

Charles Spurgeon wrote, "I venture to say that the greatest earthly blessing that God can give to any of us is health, with the possible exception of sickness.... If some men that I know of could only be favoured with a month of rheumatism, it would, by God's grace, mellow them marvelously."[8]

Though he sought to avoid suffering, Spurgeon said, "I am afraid that all the grace that I have got of my comfortable and easy times and happy hours, might almost lie on a penny. But the good that I have received from my sorrows, and pains, and griefs, is altogether incalculable."[9] Adversity and suffering can teach us who's in charge—God, not us. They remind us it's time to stop telling God what we want, and start asking God what he wants. There's relief in giving up the illusion of being God, and instead learning to trust God.

Happy are the humble.

Increased Influence

When those sharing God's Word have little personal familiarity with suffering, the credibility gap hinders them from speaking into others' lives. But our suffering levels the playing field. Through suffering we become powerless so that we might reach the powerless.

We like to serve others from the power position. We'd rather be healthy, wealthy, and wise as we reach out to the sick, poor, and ignorant. But people see and hear the gospel best when it comes through those who have known difficulty. Paul says, "To the weak I became weak, to win the weak" (1 Corinthians 9:22).

Suffering creates a sphere of influence for Christ that we couldn't otherwise have. Paul said, "It was because of an illness that I first preached the gospel to you" (Galatians 4:13). God specifically used Paul's illness to bring the gospel to Galatia.

Ron and Carol Speer, whose nine-year-old son, Kyle, died of leukemia, spent hundreds of hours in hospitals, faithfully ministering to people they never would have met without their terrible suffering. Their son's illness opened a door to ministry. God used him and them to reach many needy people. Only eternity will show the full results.

God's Glory, Our Good

Since God is the source of all goodness, his glory is the wellspring of all joy. What God does for his own sake benefits us. Therefore *whatever glorifies him is good for us.*

God explains why he takes us through difficulty: "See, I have refined you, though not as silver; I have tested you in the furnace of affliction. For my own sake, *for my own sake,* I do this" (Isaiah 48:10–11). For emphasis, God repeats the reason—for his own sake.

If you don't understand that the universe is about God and his glory—and that whatever exalts God's glory also works for your ultimate good—then you'll misunderstand this passage and countless others. Some consider God egotistical or cruel to test us for his sake. But the testing he does for *his* sake accrues to our eternal benefit.

When did you last hear someone say, "I grew closest to God when my life was free from pain and suffering"? Ease doesn't make us grow.

With so many positive results from the negative experience of suffering, no wonder the Bible tells us to "consider it pure joy... whenever you face trials of many kinds" (James 1:2). Responding properly to suffering brings a refinement that can be experienced no other way. Job says of God, "He knows the way that I take; when he has tried me, I shall come out as gold" (23:10, ESV).

Fire strengthens those it refines. There's a saying among Chinese Christians, who face suffering with remarkable faith: "True gold fears no fire."

Notes

1. Gregory A. Boyd, *Is God to Blame?* (Downers Grove, IL: InterVarsity, 2003), 55.

2. Thomas V. Morris, *Making Sense of It All* (Grand Rapids, MI: Eerdmans, 1992), 86.

3. John R. W. Stott, *The Cross of Christ* (Downers Grove, IL: InterVarsity, 1986), 327.

4. C. S. Lewis, *The Problem of Pain* (New York: Macmillan, 1962), 93.

5. Richard Baxter, *The Saints' Everlasting Rest,* ed. John Thomas Wilkinson (Grand Rapids, MI: Baker Book House, 1978), 246.

6. C. S. Lewis, *A Grief Observed* (Whitstable, Kent, UK: Whitstable Litho, 1966), 36.

7. Elisabeth Elliot, *A Path Through Suffering* (Ann Arbor, MI: Servant Publications, 1990), 154–55.

8. Charles Spurgeon, *An All-Round Ministry* (Edinburgh: The Banner of Truth Trust, 1960), 384; as cited by John Piper in his sermon "Charles Spurgeon: Preaching Through Adversity," 1995 Bethlehem Conference for Pastors (http://desiringgod.org/ResourceLibrary/Biographies/1469_Charles_Spurgeon_Preaching_Through_Adversity/).

9. Charles Spurgeon, quoted in Darrel W. Amundsen, "The Anguish and Agonies of Charles Spurgeon," in *Christian History* 10, no. 1:25; as cited by John Piper in his sermon "Charles Spurgeon: Preaching Through Adversity," 1995 Bethlehem Conference for Pastors (http://desiringgod.org/ResourceLibrary/Biographies/1469_Charles_Spurgeon_Preaching_Through_Adversity/).

11

What We Can Do

Finding Perspective in Our Suffering

Since suffering is inevitable, how can we prepare for it?

When Darrell Scott looked back at his daughter's murder at Columbine High School, he said that years before, God had prepared him. He'd read Norman Grubb's writings about the eye of faith that allows us to see through our worst circumstances to God's purpose. Most people, Darrell told me, are *look-atters*. We should learn to become *see-throughers*.

Because Darrell had learned to think this way, he could, despite his incredible pain, see through Rachel's death to a sovereign, purposeful God. Simply looking *at* the horror and apparent senselessness of Columbine would have paralyzed him, while seeing *through* it prompted him before God to carry on Rachel's heart of ministry in reaching out to others.

Darrell's view of God already had a firm place in his heart when Rachel died. He trusted from the first that God had a purpose in her death. While this did not remove his pain, it did provide solid footing from which he could move forward, trusting God instead of resenting him.

I asked Darrell what we should do to prepare for evil and suffering. Without hesitation he said, "Become a student of God's Word."

He added, "Don't be content to be hand-fed by others. Do your own reading and study, devour good books, talk about the things of God."

When suffering and evil come our way, they'll exert a force that either pushes us away from God or pulls us toward him. The perspectives we've cultivated between now and then will determine our direction. In my experience, most Christians lack grounding in God's attributes, including his sovereignty, omnipotence, omniscience, justice, and patience. We dare not wait for the time of crisis to learn perspective! The time to study these things in the Bible is *now.*

Now is the time to contemplate these words of God about the future that awaits us:

> Now the dwelling of God is with men, and he will live with them. They will be his people, and God himself will be with them and be their God. He will wipe every tear from their eyes. There will be no more death or mourning or crying or pain, for the old order of things has passed away. He who was seated on the throne said, "I am making everything new!" (Revelation 21:3–5)

RIGHT RESPONSES

But what about when we're already experiencing suffering—when it's too late to prepare, or even when we're as prepared as we could realistically be? What can we do to more fully embrace God's purposes in the midst of our ordeal?

We should realize it is *not* too late to prepare, because the time we spend today worshiping God and learning from his Word and his people *will* prepare us for tomorrow.

Based on what God has given us in Christ, we can be sure he'll give us all we need to endure evil and suffering. "He who did not spare his own Son, but gave him up for us all—how will he not also, along with him, graciously give us all things?" (Romans 8:32). When God has given us the greatest gift, the one that cost him everything, shouldn't we trust him to give us the good gifts that cost him nothing?

Trusting God for the grace to endure adversity is more an act of faith than is trusting him for deliverance from it. And we can demonstrate that trust with actions and attitudes like these:

1. Look to God's promises for comfort.

Holding on to Scripture sustains us through suffering. A woman in our church who has suffered reads her Bible each night, then hugs it as she falls asleep. She asked a pastor self-consciously, "Is that weird?" It may be unusual, but it certainly isn't weird. By clinging to God's promises, she clings to God.

In a time of dark suffering and dread, David affirmed,

> The LORD is my light and my salvation—whom shall I fear?
> The LORD is the stronghold of my life—of whom shall I be
> afraid?… Though an army besiege me, my heart will not fear;
> though war break out against me, even then will I be confi-
> dent.… Though my father and mother forsake me, the LORD
> will receive me.… I will see the goodness of the LORD in the
> land of the living. Wait for the LORD; be strong and take
> heart and wait for the LORD. (Psalm 27:1, 3, 10, 13–14)

Notice how David talks to himself about God's faithfulness and goodness, encouraging himself to wait on God. It's worth listening to self-talk if it involves speaking God's Word.

Years ago I turned off talk radio to listen to the Bible instead. Scripture, loaded on my iPod, accompanies me as I travel. I never regret investing my time this way—why listen to one more human voice when you can listen to God's?

2. Anticipate God's rewards.

Evil and suffering are temporary, but God's goodness and our joy will be eternal. Jesus told suffering believers to "rejoice...and leap for joy, because great is your reward in heaven" (Luke 6:23). Greater suffering for Christ will bring us greater eternal rewards.

The believers described in Faith's Hall of Fame (see Hebrews 11) all endured severe tests. None of them had an easy life. Yet they all clung to their belief in God's promises, trusting his goodness and believing "that He is a rewarder of those who seek Him" (verse 6, NASB).

Sadly, the doctrine of eternal rewards is one of the most neglected teachings in the Western church today, partly explaining our failure to face suffering with greater perspective and to anticipate what awaits us in Heaven.

Knowing that suffering will one day end gives us strength to endure this day. Though we don't know exactly when, we do know for sure that either by our deaths or by Christ's return, our suffering will end. From before the beginning, God drew the line in eternity's sand to say for his children, "This much and no more, then endless joy."

3. Lighten the load through prayer.

Suffering often induces stress and anxiety. If you pray in light of God's sovereign grace and unfailing love, your anxiety will eventually give way to peace. "Do not be anxious about anything, but in everything, by prayer and petition, with thanksgiving, present your requests to God. And the peace of God, which transcends all understanding, will guard your hearts and your minds in Christ Jesus" (Philippians 4:6–7).

Worry is momentary atheism crying out for correction by trust in a good and sovereign God. Paul, whom we seldom think of as vulnerable, wrote, "For we were so utterly burdened beyond our strength that we despaired of life itself. Indeed, we felt that we had received the sentence of death. But that was to make us rely not on ourselves but on God who raises the dead" (2 Corinthians 1:8–9, ESV). God uses suffering to break us of self-dependence and bring us to rely on him.

He helps us learn that he alone can bear the full weight of our pain, and give us strength and life when we feel only weakness and death. Jesus said, "Apart from me you can do nothing" (John 15:5).

Looking back at her eighteen-month-old son's death, my friend Ann Stump said, "I learned what it was like not to be able to do something on my own. I couldn't get up in the morning without the Lord's help."

4. Share your life with others who suffer.

I encourage you to get in touch with the suffering of others. Reach out to those who suffer. Give your time and energy and money to work with the poor, the unemployed, the lonely, and those who battle illnesses, disabilities, or addictions. My time spent with suffering people has been an investment not just in their lives, but also in mine.

Consider this: "The God of all comfort…comforts us in all our troubles, so that we can comfort those in any trouble with the comfort we ourselves have received from God" (2 Corinthians 1:3–4). When God uses us to help others, we discover a joy we'd never have known if we had never suffered.

A Final Word

This Changes Everything

I f I had to believe that what we now see around us represents God's best for this world, I wouldn't be a Christian. If not for the redemptive work of Christ, I wouldn't believe in God's goodness. The fault would lie with me, for God would remain good even if Jesus hadn't gone to the cross for us. But no matter how persuasive the argument that we sinners deserve judgment, I couldn't overcome the obstacles of suffering children, the Holocaust, or the Killing Fields.

But the way I look at suffering and evil and their reflection on God's character is transformed by the fact that Jesus Christ, the eternal Son of God, chose to endure the holocaust of the Cross to pay for sin—that he deliberately took upon himself the evil and suffering of all people in Golgotha's killing field.

The proven character of Christ, demonstrated in his sacrifice on our behalf, makes him trustworthy in the face of the worst evil and suffering.

For me, Jesus changes everything.

FIXED FOCUS

When we feel upset with God and are tempted to blame him, we should look at the outstretched arms of Jesus and focus on *his* wounds, not ours.

When we lock our eyes on our cancer, arthritis, fibromyalgia, diabetes, or disability, self-pity and bitterness can creep in. When we spend our days rehearsing the tragic death of a loved one, we'll interpret all life through the darkness of our suffering.

How much better when we focus upon Jesus!

"Let us fix our eyes on Jesus…who for the joy set before him endured the cross." The following verse commands us, "Consider him who endured such opposition from sinful men, so that you will not grow weary and lose heart" (Hebrews 12:2–3). However great our suffering, *his* was far greater.

If you feel angry at God, what price would you have him pay for his failure to do more for people facing suffering and evil? Would you inflict capital punishment on him? You're too late. No matter how bitter we feel toward God, could any of us come up with a punishment worse than what God chose to inflict upon himself?

Tim Keller writes,

> If we again ask the question: "Why does God allow evil and suffering to continue?" and we look at the cross of Jesus, we still do not know what the answer is. However, we know what the answer isn't. It can't be that he doesn't love us. It can't be that he is indifferent or detached from our condition. God takes our misery and suffering so seriously that he was willing to take it on himself.[1]

One day when we stand before Christ, having wondered at times whether he really cared about us, perhaps we'll see him extend his nail-scarred hands to us and ask a pointed question: "Do these look like the hands of a God who doesn't care?"

Seeing for Yourself

In this book I've explained my conviction that the Christian world-view best answers the problem of evil and suffering. Still, God doesn't force the Christian faith on anyone.

But don't rely on what I say or anyone else says about Jesus. See him for yourself.

"Come and see what God has done, how awesome his works in man's behalf!" (Psalm 66:5).

Scripture gives us many such invitations to come to God and personally experience him. The best way to do this is to open the Bible. Set aside all other arguments and study the person of Christ. Read his story in the Gospels, the books of Matthew, Mark, Luke, and John.

Listen to him. Can you look at Jesus and not be pierced? Can you see how he loved people and not be broken? Can you hear his words and not thirst for the One who spoke them? Can you gaze on the crucified Christ and still resent God for not doing enough to show his love?

Ask God to mercifully open your eyes and reveal to you this Jesus you read about. Once you see Jesus as he really is, your world-view, your goals, your affections, *everything*—including your view of evil and suffering—will change.

Jesus asked his disciples the most important question: *"Who do you say I am?"* (Matthew 16:15). If we get it right about Jesus, we can afford to get some minor things wrong. But if we get it wrong about Jesus, it won't matter in the end what else we get right.

The Pulled Switch

As a young Christian I heard a pastor use the illustration of a railroad switch operator who brought his beloved son to work with him. At one point he saw two trains coming from opposite directions on the same track. He could avoid the collision only by throwing a switch so one train moved to other tracks—but he looked up to see his boy playing on those very tracks. If he didn't pull the switch, hundreds of people would die. If he did, just one would die—his only son.

The train operator pulled the switch. As he saw his son crushed, through his tears he watched hundreds of people pass, clueless to the sacrifice he had just made on their behalf.

Likewise, many of us remain oblivious or indifferent to God's sacrifice of his only Son to preserve us from destruction and to purchase for us eternal life.

If you feel angry with a God you claim doesn't exist, denying him may be your revenge—but it's *you* who'll end up suffering for it. Whether you bow to him now in love or later in judgment, every knee *will* bow to him (see Philippians 2:10–11).

Sure and Secure

Steve Saint told me about the day he and his wife, Ginny, eagerly waited to meet their daughter, twenty-year-old Stephenie, at the airport after she returned from a long trip. With the Saints stood Mincaye, one of the tribal warriors who, in 1956, had murdered five missionaries in Ecuador, including Steve's father, Nate. Eventually the gospel Mincaye's victims had brought to him transformed him. Mincaye became part of the Saint family, the children calling him

Grandfather. At the airport, Grandfather Mincaye waved a sign (upside down) that read Welcome Home, Stephenie.

That night, in the midst of their celebration, Stephenie developed a headache and asked Steve to pray for her. Ginny sat on the bed and held Stephenie, while Steve put his arms around both of them and started praying. While he prayed, Stephenie suffered a massive cerebral hemorrhage. They rushed her to the hospital, where Mincaye saw his beloved Stephenie, whom he called Star, lying on a gurney with a tube down her throat and needles in her arm. He grabbed Steve and asked, "Who did this to her?"

"I don't know, Mincaye. Nobody is doing this."

Mincaye grabbed Steve again and said, "Babae, don't you see? *God himself is doing this.*"

Excitedly, Mincaye addressed all the people in the emergency room: "Don't you see? God loving Star; he's taking her to live with him."

Then he told them, "Look at me, I'm an old man; pretty soon I'm going to die too, and I'm going there."

Finally, with a pleading look on his face, Mincaye exhorted these bystanders, "Please, please, won't you follow God's trail too? Coming to God's place, Star and I will be waiting there to welcome you."

Within a few hours, Stephenie died. I'm confident that when she left this world, a celebration erupted in a better world, where others, including her Lord and her grandfather Nate Saint, whom she'd never met, stretched out their arms and said, "Welcome home, Stephenie."

Don't you long for that kind of celebration, for God to say to you on the other side of death, "Welcome home, my child"? Do you wonder if it's really possible to know this in advance? The Bible tells us we *can* know for sure that our death will bring the end of our suffering and usher us into eternal life in the presence of Jesus: "I write these things to you who believe in the name of the Son of God so *that you may know* that you have eternal life" (1 John 5:13).

GOOD NEWS

Here's a summary of what God calls the gospel or "the good news":

Sin has terrible consequences, but God has provided a solution: "The wages of sin is death, but the gift of God is eternal life in Christ Jesus our Lord" (Romans 6:23).

Jesus lived a sinless life (see Hebrews 2:17–18; 4:15–16) and died to pay the penalty for our sins (see 2 Corinthians 5:21). On the cross, he took upon himself the Hell we deserve, in order to purchase for us the Heaven we don't deserve. When he died, he said, "It is finished" (John 19:30), using the Greek word for canceling certificates of debt; it meant "paid in full." Jesus then rose from the grave, defeating sin and conquering death (see 1 Corinthians 15:3–4, 54–57).

How many routes can take us to the Father in Heaven? Peter declared, "Salvation is found in no one else [but Jesus], for there is no other name under heaven given to men by which we must be saved" (Acts 4:12). Jesus said, "I am *the* way and *the* truth and *the* life. No one comes to the Father *except through me*" (John 14:6). That's an exclusive statement, but Jesus made it. Do you believe him?

God freely offers us forgiveness in Christ: "He does not treat us as our sins deserve or repay us according to our iniquities.... As far as the east is from the west, so far has he removed our transgressions from us" (Psalm 103:10, 12). To be forgiven, we must repent of our unbelief and whatever sins God brings to our minds: "If we confess our sins, he is faithful and just and will forgive us our sins and purify us from all unrighteousness" (1 John 1:9).

"If you confess with your mouth, 'Jesus is Lord,' and believe in your heart that God raised him from the dead, you will be saved" (Romans 10:9).

FREE GIFT

Righteous deeds will not earn us a place in Heaven (see Titus 3:5). We can take no credit for salvation: "For it is by grace you have been saved, through faith—and this not from yourselves, it is the gift of God—not by works, so that no one can boast" (Ephesians 2:8–9).

Christ offers to everyone the gift of forgiveness and eternal life: "Whoever is thirsty, let him come; and whoever wishes, let him take the free gift of the water of life" (Revelation 22:17).

If you haven't accepted this gift offered by Christ—at such a great price to him—what's stopping you?

If you do not humble yourself before God to recognize your inability to deliver yourself from your evil and suffering, what will become of you?

If you do not reach out and gratefully receive the gift of Christ's atoning suffering on behalf of your sins, what hope do you have to escape eternal punishment?

Why not ask God to give you the heart and desire to reach out to him and receive his gift of eternal life?

Why not put your faith in him, and ask him to make you his child so you can joyfully worship and serve him in a redeemed universe, bought and paid for by his own blood?

"To all who received him [Jesus], to those who believed in his name, he gave the right to become children of God" (John 1:12).

Note
1. Timothy Keller, *The Reason for God* (New York: Dutton, 2008), 31.

You can discover much more about the issues discussed here by reading Randy Alcorn's definitive book *If God Is Good: Faith in the Midst of Suffering and Evil.* It's available for purchase at your local bookstore or at www.epm.org.

You can connect with the author and his organization at:

Eternal Perspective Ministries
39085 Pioneer Boulevard, Suite 206
Sandy, OR 97055
503-668-5200

www.epm.org
www.randyalcorn.blogspot.com
www.facebook.com/randyalcorn
www.twitter.com/randyalcorn

If you don't have a church home that is Christ-centered and teaches the Bible, and need help finding one, contact the author's ministry at info@epm.org. If we can make some recommendations, we will.

Delve deep into suffering, evil, and God's goodness

Randy Alcorn diligently tackles the toughest questions about suffering, evil and the goodness of God to uncover the hopeful truth from the only reliable source—the Bible. Increase your understanding of this complex topic and equip yourself to share your faith more clearly in this world of pain and fear.

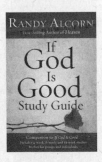

Special introductory booklet, available as a 10-pack. Randy Alcorn takes on the key questions we can't escape when we search for God amidst the suffering and evil before us. Ideal for distribution to grief support group members or as a gift for a loved one struggling with loss.

Three study guides in one.
* The four-week study is an overview of the key points of *If God Is Good* and how they reveal a character of God that is loving and comforting in times of trouble.
* The eight-week study is an advanced course that probes the theological arguments in *If God Is Good,* including the sovereignty of God, the problem of evil, and the existence of God.
* The thirteen-week study is structured for use as a church sermon series and Sunday school discussions.
* Includes Leaders' guide.